"'Guts' and 'manhood' - words that speak directly to my heart. In NFL locker rooms, guts and manhood are constantly spoken of, questioned, and on display. But what about the locker room of your life? Your job, your relationships, and most importantly – your family? In *Guts and Manhood,* Jim Ramos clearly lays out how to break out of the daily grind and build into your life attributes that all men aspire to: fearlessness, strength, and courage. Buck the male passivity that permeates our culture and become the courageous leader of your locker room once again. *Guts and Manhood*: if this book doesn't get you fired up – it's time to check your pulse!"

Brent Jones
San Francisco Forty-Niners Tight End
Three-Time Super Bowl Champ
Four-Time All-Pro Tight End

"Jim has done a masterful job with this power-packed book. Like a skilled prize fighter, Jim delivers a direct blow to the issues facing men. After the knockout punch, he picks you up and helps you get ready for the next battle. Well done, Jim...well done!"

Rod Handley
Founder and President of Character that Counts

———

"Jim Ramos is the consummate expert on living a courageous life, and his new book, *Guts and Manhood* is a game-changer for any man who desires to engage every battle in his life with proven biblical tactics. Whether you're facing a life-or-death challenge, or just trying to survive day-to-day life, let *Guts and Manhood* be your 'battle buddy' as you hit life head on. You will emerge victorious!"

David Dusek
Founder and Executive Director of
Rough Cut Men Ministries
Author of Amazon #1 bestselling "Rough Cut Men" and
"The Battle"

HERO STORIES

"The endorsements from experts in manhood that you just read are right - this is a great book. But wouldn't you rather hear from the real heroes? These are men just like you who are getting it done in the arena of life, growing into their best version, and celebrating their battle stories with us.

Enjoy what we call our 'Hero Stories' - stories from men and women around the world who have been impacted by the principles laid out in this book. If you send us your story, you might see your name here someday!"

"I just want to weep at how beautiful the ministry of Men in the Arena is. Your podcast should be listened to by women also so we can get out of the way of our men being men. Thank you for the mighty influence you have had on my husband."

MELANIE, OREGON

"Men in the Arena has helped me understand how to be a better husband. My wife and I have been struggling in our marriage for a few years, and just recently she was seeing another man and almost left me. She has ended that relationship and is committed to making our marriage work. I have learned a lot and am on the path to be a better Christian man, husband, and father."

AUSTIN, WASHINGTON

"Men in the Arena has had a huge impact on my life. Your ministry has become an important part of my pursuit of becoming a godly man. I feel that the resources I get from you allow me to see Jesus Christ as a manly man. This radically changes my view of Christianity. Now, I feel proud to be a follower of Jesus because, through you, I can develop and cultivate my own masculinity towards biblical principles."

MIROSLAV, CZECH REPUBLIC

"I'm a drastically different man now than I was a year ago and your ministry is a huge part of that! The only reason I didn't quit my current job 6 month ago is because I get to work with headphones in and listen to the podcast. Ha!"

TONY, WASHINGTON

"God used Men in the Arena to completely change the trajectory of my life and marriage. Everything looked really good on the outside, but I had pushed my wife far away in my heart. Over the last four months I've made some drastic change and I wanted you to know your ministry was the spark that opened me up to what was really going on inside of me."

BRADY, IDAHO

"I have been a pastor over 40 years and I am still learning and being challenged by your ministry. God bless you."

FRANK, WASHINGTON

"I am truly honored to be mentioned on the show. I cannot express my gratitude enough for how your message has shaped my walk with the Lord."

JOSH, ILLINOIS

"Men in the Arena has been a lighthouse of inspiration to me the last few years! The tools presented through your podcast and actual meetings have given me the inspiration to return God's pursuance. Besides my relationship with Jesus, Men in the Arena has inspired me to be a better husband and father also! I share your podcasts and material like its gold and love listening in the office (loudly). Your material changed me and I'm reading through it again before I give it away."

CODY, WYOMING

"The 17–20-year-old boys in the group home I run listen to your podcast as we ruck. Most come from hard places: usually fatherlessness, poverty and the foster care system. I tell them, 'You had a rough start that was outside of your control, but now it's time to be a man and that's only in your hands.' You're doing powerful things, thanks for letting me use you from afar to shape corners of heaven!"

CJ, MISSISSIPPI

"Thank you for helping my husband become a man. We live 90 miles from the nearest box store, and it's always been a stressful trip because my husband doesn't do well driving in traffic. He yells, gives hand gestures, swears and it's common for us to be in a complete mess when we arrive. He's constantly telling me to 'hurry up' when we shop, and I'm always at least 15-20 feet behind him. Today was different—incredible. No angry driving issues. He waited for me and walked **with** me, which was a first. He was helpful, kind, and irresistible. I was getting turned on but was skeptical because—quite frankly— this was **NOT** my husband. Today my husband was the gentlest I've ever seen him. THANK YOU for helping him! Men in the Arena has made a difference in his life, which had made a difference in my life."

AMY, WYOMING

"I was scrolling through my social media feed and stumbled upon this post about Matthew 5:38-42, about turning the other cheek. I can't thank you enough for this perspective. It's given me some fresh clarity on this topic, especially as a new father. It has been an afterthought looming in the back of my head on how I will teach my son during the challenging times. Thank you!"

BILL, RHODE ISLAND

"I just heard your podcast about how your wife is **not** your best friend. What a kick in the face. I've always said that she was-like you-but what you say is completely accurate. She does not see me necessarily in the same way. Have a great weekend and keep fighting the good fight! We appreciate you."

BRANDON, MISSOURI

"In June 2021, I had a stroke. While I was recovering, I had the time to read *Strong Men Dangerous Times.* God used your book to help me put things back into alignment. The Men in the Arena forum and the podcasts have been very good for my growth as well. I am now 279 days away from retirement. I am now more focused on who I will be in retirement and not just what will I do in retirement."

DOUG, CALIFORNIA

"Thankful this morning for you guys, and that I pulled the trigger on registering for this group. I have communicated more with all of you than I have in other groups that are in person. Have a great day everyone."

NATIONAL VIRTUAL TEAM MEMBER

"I just got your free *Tell Them* book and read through it in the first couple of days. Great topics to talk about with my sons! So meaningful! I find it is another area I fall short on. I give my kids a lot of affection but don't do well on meaningful conversation. This is a great tool. It has already provoked thoughts about how I can improve on how my father spent time with me. Thank you!"

"TROCCO" VIA INSTAGRAM

"I love your podcasts. I am working my way through them. I started at the beginning, and am currently on episode 255. Love them! I am in the middle of the Arena, getting hit from all sides!!! Your podcast is different than the other podcasts I listen to. You are down to earth and do not sugar coat things. Thank you for keeping it real!!"

DAVE, PENNSYLVANIA

"I was searching for podcasts concerning men's issues and growing closer to Jesus. I found your podcast and have been listening for the last few years. Your ministry has been a big part of my spiritual growth, it has truly been a blessing. I appreciate all you do! Thank you."

BRYAN, INDIANA

"I'm Brazilian and I listen to your podcast here! It's been so helpful. God bless you. I'm a husband and a father, and one of the most challenging things I face is to find someone to walk with, to share the struggles, and so on. So, I try to do this by podcasts and sermons on the internet."

PABLO, BRAZIL

"A friend shared a podcast you did recently about legacy, and did that hit home. I am a dad who wants nothing more than to be a better parent and husband. It seems every job I have had consumes me to the point there is not much left of me. I am at a crossroads and trying to figure out what's next. I thank you for your message as it made a difference today. It put a little fight back in me. I have been beat up so much there's not much left. I too hope I can find my purpose."

GREG, OKLAHOMA

"I wasn't a good husband or father, and it was showing in my wife's birthday smile circa 2015. A week later she took the kids and left me for almost 70 days. I was a cheating, lying, chain-smoking, alcoholic. If I was her, I would have done the same thing. During that time I got connected with a Men in the Arena small group and started listening to the podcast. On one episode you said, 'pray with your wife,' and that was a game-changer. My wife moved back, and you should see her smile now! Our marriage is stronger now than ever!"

ALEX, OREGON

"Thank you for your ministry and the impact it has had in my life. Without any guidance from an older man in my life, I have been struggling. Then I found Men in the Arena and things changed. Thanks to your ministry I now have a source for continued teaching and encouragement. In the last two years that I have been following Men in the Arena I have grown in my faith and been able to help my family grow as well. I have learned to 'make decisions against myself' and consistently get up earlier so I can read my Bible and pray. I have a much better picture of what I need to do going forward to be the best version of myself and to lead my family. Thanks again for all you do for guys like me."

SETH, OREGON

GUTS AND MANHOOD

FOUR IRREFUTABLE ATTRIBUTES OF COURAGE

JIM RAMOS

Five
Stones
Press

COPYRIGHT

© 2021 **Jim Ramos**

Publisher: Five Stones Press, Dallas, Texas

For quantity sales, textbooks, and orders by trade bookstores or wholesalers contact Five Stones Press at publish@fivestonespress.net

Five Stones Press is owned and operated by Five Stones Church, a nonprofit 501c3 religious organization. Press name and logo are trademarked. Contact publisher for use.

Jim Ramos's website is www.meninthearena.org - Men in the Arena can bring speakers to your organization to teach the principles covered in this book.

All chapter entries are listed in order according to where they appear in Scripture. Unless noted the entries are from the New American Standard Bible (NASB).

Printed in the United States of America

FOREWORD

"Men in the Arena army. We salute you!"

This book is dedicated to every man who is fighting for his faith, wife, children, and community. You are the true heroes in this world. This world wins because you get it. You are the few, the humble, the courageous—the Men in the Arena.

"Be strong and very courageous."

— GOD, JOSHUA 1:7

Acknowledgement

A special Thank You to Ken Watson, for your diligent work on this project. Your tenaciousness is inspiring!

Books for Your Journey

- *Tell Them: What Great Fathers Tell Their Sons and Daughters (Free Download at www.meninthearena.org)*
- *The Field Guide: A Bathroom Book for Men*
- *Strong Men Dangerous Times: Five Essentials Every Man Must Possess to Change His World*
- *Guts and Manhood: Four Irrefutable Attributes of Courage*

Books for Locking Shields

- *Strong Men Series—The Trailhead: Protecting Integrity*
- *Strong Men Series—The Climb: Fighting Apathy*
- *Strong Men Series—The Summit: Pursuing God Passionately*
- *Strong Men Series—The Descent: Leading Courageously*
- *Strong Men Series—The Trail's End: Finishing Strong*

Courage is grace under pressure.

— ERNEST HEMINGWAY (1899-1961)

TABLE OF CONTENTS

He who is brave is free.

— SENECA (4 BC-65 AD)

Gut Check

*And they brought to Him a paralytic lying on a bed. Seeing their faith, Jesus said to the paralytic, "**Take courage**, son; your sins are forgiven."*
Matthew 9:2

"I learned that courage was not the absence of fear, but the triumph over it. The brave man is not he who does not feel afraid, but he who conquers that fear."
—Nelson Mandela (1918–2013)

*But Jesus turning and seeing her said, "Daughter, **take courage**; your faith has made you well."*
Matthew 9:22

"Courage isn't having the strength to go on—
it is going on when you don't have strength."
—Napoleon Bonaparte (1789–1821)

On the bookshelf in my office sits my only remaining trophy, the rest were destroyed years ago as a ministry demonstration. It remains because it spoke about my character more than athletic ability. When I destroyed my trophies, long story, this one remained as a monument to a lifelong journey of growing guts and glory.

In 1988, my Santa Clara University teammates voted me the Most Courageous man on the team for disregarding doctor's orders to end my career due to a paralysis-threatening neck injury between my c5-c6 vertebrae. No wonder they called us Full "blocks" instead of Fullbacks! All that remains from that season are fond memories, that trophy, and Stage Three Kidney Disease from a three-month prescription of 2,400 milligrams per day of Ibuprofen (hey, I was invincible).

This book is the product of my personal struggle against cowardice to remain a man of gutsy fortitude—courage. It is an exhaustive study of the word "courage" through my personal Bible study, and subsequent journey towards courage. In late 2002 I sensed a major life event was looming and that I would need courage to press into it. I determined to journal everything the Bible taught about courage. This book is little more than those handwritten journal entries transcribed into book form.

It was a gut check.

What I discovered about it was life-changing for me and it will be for you as well.

Don't be fooled because of the book size. Its contents gave me the guts to follow God's leading (along with my bride of only ten years) and pack up my three young sons, a herd of pets, and leave our family, friends, and hometown.

With our life packed into a moving truck, we moved our frightened family nearly 1,000 miles to McMinnville, Oregon, where we had only been once, for the pastoral position interview. It was the toughest decision of our lives.

It was a gut check moment.

A decade later it happened again after receiving God's call to quit my day job as a pastor and launch a faith-based, non-profit organization from scratch, which you know as Men in the Arena. I dove headlong into the courage journals from a decade earlier, and again they inspired me onward. But I'll never forget those heart racing nights of terror, wrestling with how to earn an income where one no longer existed. Where would we live once our house was taken from us by the bank, which was weeks away from happening? How embarrassing would it look to lick our wounds, pack up our belongings, and leave the town we loved?

Would I trust God for he impossible? Yet another gut check.

This book is from my guts. It's packed with emotion. It's personal. It's me wrestling with my fears. I hope you can sense those gutty growth pains as you read along. Between the New American Standard and New International Version translations of the Bible, courage, or a derivative thereof, is mentioned 57 times, many of which are redundancics. For example, "be strong and courageous" is mentioned over a dozen times throughout. I've tried to include as many Bible verses as possible on courage without boring you with repetitiveness, which is why you'll discover not all passages are referenced in this book.

Lastly, *Guts and Manhood* is divided into four major

sections. Do not ignore this. It's the guts (forgive the pun) of the book and essence of my discovery about courage—what it is and is not. Courage is essentially four things: 1) call to action, 2) personal choice, 3) sign of strength, and 4) character trait over time.

My prayer is that this book inspires you towards great things as it did me. Men are wired for courage, but we need to understand it on a biblical level. I challenge you to take an honest look at yourself. It's about time for a gut check. Enjoy the ride.

CHAPTER 1

COURAGE: THE HUNT FOR GOLD

The eyes of the Lord move to and fro
throughout the earth that He may strongly support those
whose heart is completely His.
2 Chronicles 16:9

"The credit belongs to the man who is actually in the arena, whose face is marred by dust and sweat and blood; who strives **valiantly**; who errs, who comes short again and again, because there is no effort without error and shortcoming; but who does actually strive to do the deeds; who knows great enthusiasms, the great devotions; who spends himself in a worthy cause; who at the best knows in the end the triumph of high achievement, and who at the worst, if he fails, at least fails while daring greatly, so that his place shall never be with those cold and timid souls who neither know victory nor defeat."
—Theodore Roosevelt (1858-1919)

I walked onto the main stage with over four hundred men staring back at me. It was an honor to stand with the half dozen presenters representing as many states. "No pressure Jim. You'd better bring your 'A' Game. These guys have never heard of you," I thought as something caught my eye.

Approaching the podium, the screen above flashed a new slide that stopped me in my tracks: "Jim Ramos, Gresham, Oregon: Hunt for Gold."

I nervously laughed out loud. "For the record," I spoke into the microphone, "I live in McMinnville, not Gresham, and we're The Great Hunt for **God** not Hunt for Gold!"

When I commented on the mistake, the conference leader bluntly responded, "Close enough!"

I proceeded to give my best pitch, had two standing-room-only seminars, and sold all of our resources. On the way home I silently laughed, remembering a Christian leader who said, "There's gold in them thar pews."

The Great Hunt for God, now Men in the Arena, is on a hunt for treasure more valuable than gold. We are looking for people who share our passion for men to become their best version in Christ because when a man gets it—everyone wins.

We're looking for full capacity men who care about their spiritual fire more than about the world's paper fire lies. We're in a manhood crisis and must act now if we're going to climb out of the indifference—forgive me, opposition—our culture displays towards true masculinity.

I have a close friend who was a gold miner for years. No kidding. He spent millions of dollars on space-aged equipment in order to pull every ounce of gold from the claim. Unlike our visions of a 19th century gold miner stooped over a High Sierra stream with his mining pan, this was a huge operation in high desert of eastern Oregon. Most of the gold was barely larger than a grain of sand.

The details about how gold is mined remind me of how God searches, mining for men who are unwilling to bend to this neutered brand of pseudo masculinity; *"The eyes of the Lord move to and fro throughout the earth that He may strongly support those whose heart is completely His"* (*2 Chronicles 16:9).*

There's gold out there but it's disguised in men wearing blue jeans, T-shirts, and work boots. The treasure is hidden—in you! His mission is buried within every man waiting for the moment when that man courageously steps out in faith and begs God, "Put me on display!"

Don't hesitate. Let God's fire blaze through you!

Gut Check
Small Group Exercise

Ernest Hemingway, who committed suicide in 1961, is credited with saying, "Courage is grace under pressure."

What tensions do you see between being a man of courage and battling your demons?

How does 2 Chronicles 16:1-10 speak to us about courage. What can you take away from this story?

Seneca (4 BC-65 AD) said, "He who is brave is free." What does this mean?

Where are you not free today?

Matthew 14:22-33 records Jesus walking on water. In verse 27 he said to them, *"Take courage! It is I. Don't be afraid."*

Where do you need to hear his words today?

What is your greatest fear?

CHAPTER 2

COURAGE: AGAINST THE WIND

*And he **took courage** and rebuilt all the wall that had been broken down and erected towers on it, and built another outside wall and strengthened the Millo in the city of David, and made weapons and shields in great number.*
2 Chronicles 32:5

"**Courage** is being scared to death, but saddling up anyway."
—John Wayne (1907–1979)

*These things I have spoken to you, so that in Me you may have peace. In the world you have tribulation, but **take courage**; I have overcome the world."*
John 16:33

AS A YOUNG BOY, OUR FAMILY VACATIONED AT Nevada's Wild Horse Reservoir. We rented a motor home and started out epic journey, but our vacation went south as each of us kids got a severe case of chicken pox. To add insult to injury the Winnebago had all sorts of problems, and we were thankful to make it home in one piece —barely.

But the trout fishing was epic, and along with the pox, I will never forget trolling those brown Wooly Buggers that giant rainbows devoured.

Have you ever had a vacation that fell way short of your expectations? How about your life? Is your life not what you signed up for? Do you wish you had a second chance?

Unfortunately, we live in a world where marriages fail, loved ones get sick, people lose their jobs, and people disappoint. The storms of life wash away many of our childhood hopes and dreams while the clouds of adversity cover the rays of the sun. Sin crushes the dreams of youth and progress is stalled because *"the wind was against us."*

Life is more often like the Bob Segar hit song, *Against the Wind.* No matter what we do, sometimes the wind is contrary. Sometimes we can't do enough to keep the wind from knocking us down. It's in these storms that we are tempted to lose sight of the other side of our dreams. We lose sight of the calming voice of Jesus intervening, "Hush, be still."

Our Savior has the power to still even the fiercest storm.

Fighting against the wind, the last person the disciples expected to see in the darkness was **Jesus** walking on water.

But there he was! In their face, challenging them to face their fears.

Life is hard. Life is harsh. Life is harassing at times. It can feel unforgiving, and during those times we need the courage to call on the one who still calms storms. When least expected, there He was coming to their rescue, *"Take courage! It is I. Don't be afraid."*

He still calms storms.

He still calms storms.

Gut Check
Small Group Exercise

Read Mark 4:35-41. Where do you feel like you are fighting against the wind?

What is standing in opposition to you?

In John 16:33 and Philippians 4:6-7 we read about the peace of Christ.

How do you find peace during the storm?

What disrupts your peace?

What things should you avoid to maintain peace?

Read 2 Chronicles 32:1-8 but focus on verse 5. What does "took courage" mean to you?

What does it reveal about the nature of courage?

CHAPTER 3

COURAGE: MYTHS AND MISCONCEPTIONS

"**Courage** is not simply one of the virtues but the form of every virtue at the testing point, which means at the point of highest reality."
—C.S. Lewis (1898–1963)

"**Courage** is like love, it must have hope for nourishment."
—Napoleon Bonaparte (1769–1821)

"An unbelieved truth can hurt a man much more than a lie. It takes great **courage** to back truth unacceptable to our times. There's a punishment for it, and it's usually crucifixion."
—John Steinbeck (1902–1968)

*"**Take courage**; it is I, do not be afraid."*
—JESUS, Mark 6:50

I'm proud of my bestselling book, *Strong Men Dangerous Times* that guides men towards their best version by clearly identifying what a man truly is. It is the best book I've ever seen on clearly, definitively defining manhood and should be in every man's library (if I do say so myself!) In it I unpack five essentials of manhood after unpacking several myths and misconceptions about masculinity.

According to Google Dictionary a myth is, "a traditional or legendary story, usually concerning some hero or event, with or without a determinable basis of fact or a natural explanation, and explains some practice, rite, or phenomenon of nature."

Google defines a misconception as, "a wrong or inaccurate idea."

Here are six myths and misconceptions about manhood discussed in *Strong Men Dangerous Times*. First, **manhood is defined by a job or title**. What's one of the first questions between men?

"What do you do?"

Your career is not who you are. With the urbanization of America during the Industrial Revolution of the early 1900's people flocked to the cities and women entered the work force in a non-agrarian role. World War II solidified this when women were compelled to work in the factories as the men fought the war. In the past one hundred years, we've moved from a traditional family structure where the husband worked in a career while the wife was the full-time homemaker. Today we see a much more egalitarian model where spouses share the work and household loads. But this has created confusion for men, who for centuries identified who they were as men with what they did. In many households today, not only does the wife work but she's the primary wage earner. Can you see how this impacts a man's identity?

Second, a man is not his **financial portfolio.** The ability to make money and the ability to act as a man are different. They are often bipolar. We wrongly assume that the rich somehow have it together, but all that wealth does is mask the deeper problems. Think about the twenty-two-year-old who is a multimillionaire simply because he can run fast, jump high, or throw a ball accurately. To think that young male is a man because he can afford an agent is ignorance at best.

Wealth and status make it easier to cover deeper issues and hide them behind the cloud of money. Think about the rich and famous. Do they have it together? Do movie stars we watch live like the characters they portray in the movies they make? No, because it's fiction! Most are nothing more than dressed up train wrecks.

Let me throw another truth into the mix. Did I mention that Jesus was never elevated in Scripture because of his great carpentry skills? Did you know that Jesus was strategically homeless for at least three or four years of his life? Of himself he proclaimed, *"Foxes have dens and birds have nests, but the Son of Man has no place to lay his head" (Matthew 8:20).* Clearly, wealth does not mean that one man is better than another.

Third, a man is not his **talents** and **abilities.** When vacationing in Mexico we ran into a newlywed couple at poolside. I soon learned that the husband worked for a professional baseball scouting company, specializing in pitchers.

I learned first-hand that the only thing separating college football athletes from Division I, II or III is not heart, skill, or intelligence. It's often simply a game of metrics—height, weight, and speed.

I noticed that most Major League Baseball pitchers are tall and have a long reach and stride. I asked if similar metrics applied for baseball and he not only affirmed my assumption but took it to the next level.

"We actually use a mathematical equation based on arm length, stride, and height. We can determine with a high level of accuracy the maximum output (speed) potential of a young pitcher. If he's too short, for example, we will barely give him a look because his maximum output won't be high enough. It's a metrics game. Drive and determination have little to do with our recruiting. Everyone has that."

Think about this. If your metrics are exceptional along with throwing accuracy, you can be a twenty-year-old millionaire who is on television commercials, is famous, and has thousands of fans cheering every time you step on the mound.

But it doesn't make you a man. The genetics to meet a mathematical standard and throw an accurate 100-mile-an-hour fastball only makes you a good pitcher. It just means you can throw things fast, accurately, and make a lot of money.

Your family, friends, and God are way more in need of a good man than they are of good metrics!

Fourth, manhood doesn't happen at a certain **age**. Chronology does not equate to manhood. Action does. A man is as a man does. Almost daily I witness forty, fifty, and sixty-year-old men who are males but not men. They are boys masquerading in men's bodies. Awhile back a man entered a building without his wife, and I wondered out loud, "I haven't seen his wife at church lately."

The 80-year-old man next to me matter-of-factly stated, "He's divorcing her because she's a slob. Do you blame him?"

"Yes, I do! He's a male but not a man and neither are you for making that comment," I refrained myself from saying.

Fifth, a man is not his **anatomy.** Just as reaching the age of pubic hair does not turn a male into a man neither does having a penis. Men aren't born. Babies are born. Children are raised. But men, oh men, they're forged in the fires of responsibility, compounded daily over time. A man is made. And after he's been made, a man acts like a man.

Lastly, and the most important myth we must dispel is that somehow **"looking" like a man** makes one so. Let me explain. A strong man is not about his image, it's about his actions. Have I said this before? We have a hugely mistaken stereotype that a man is built, talks, and dresses a certain way. Just because he is built like a bodybuilder, wears flannel with his jeans and boots, drives a big truck, and swings an ax for a living means nothing. Some of the weakest, most childish, men I know have looked like tough guys. I have a suggestion for all you tough guys out there.

Stop trying to act like a strong man and start living like one.

Similar to the six myths and misconceptions surrounding manhood, there are at least three misconceptions that Jesus followers need to learn about biblical courage. Let me explain.

Courage is not a spiritual gift. In 1 Corinthians 12:1-30, 14:1-39, and Romans 12:1-8, Paul spent a great deal of time explaining the spiritual gifts. I have taken dozens of spiritual gifts tests over the years and have never seen "courage" listed among them. It simply is not there because it is not a gift God gives to His followers. It sounds weird admitting this but it's true. God never gave the gift of courage to anyone in the Bible—ever. This book references every time the word *courage* is mentioned the New American Standard (NASB) or New International Version (NIV) translations of the Bible. I encourage you to check to see if you can find more time *courage* in mentioned in your Bible translation.

He didn't give it to Abraham. He didn't give it to Noah. He didn't give it to David. He didn't give it to Solomon. He didn't give it Samson. He didn't give it to Peter. He didn't give it to Paul. And he definitely didn't give it to our Savior, Jesus.

It is a misinterpretation of Scripture to claim it as such.

Courage is not a fruit of the Spirit. This is much simpler to explain because there is only one reference to fruits of the Spirit. In Galatians 5:22-23 Paul lists nine, *"But the fruit of the Spirit is love, joy, peace, patience, kindness, goodness, faithfulness, gentleness, self-control; against such things there is no law."*

One could argue, however, that Paul identifies two more fruits of the Spirit in Ephesians 5:8-9, adding "righteousness" and "truth" to the list; "for you were formerly darkness, but now you are Light in the Lord; walk as children of Light (for the fruit of the Light *consists* in all goodness and righteousness and truth)."

But again, courage is nowhere to be found.

In fact, of the 238 mentions of the word "fruit" in the New American Standard Bible, "fruit (s) of the Spirit" is only mentioned one other time, *"But also we ourselves, having the first fruits of the Spirit, even we ourselves groan within ourselves, waiting eagerly for our adoption as sons, the redemption of our body"* (Romans 8:23).

Courage is not a fruit of the Spirit.

Courage is not among the Ten Commandments. Of all of the things God could have commanded His people to do in Exodus 20:1-17, one would think living courageous lives would be among them. Men in the Arena was launched out of the last church I worked at, Church on the Hill in McMinnville, Oregon where our vison was, "Courageously following Christ."

And I loved it. I helped craft it, even though God never listed it among His Ten Commandments. In fact, when asked which was the greatest Commandment, I am sure that courage was far from his mind when he answered, *"'You shall love the Lord your God with all your heart, and with all your soul, and with all your mind.' This is the great and foremost commandment"* (Matthew 22:36-40).

Then why is courage vital to the Christian faith? Why were some of the bravest people in human history followers of Jesus who were courageously martyred? Before the

Apostle Paul was beheaded for his faith, he issued a warning to all who follow Jesus: "*Indeed, all who desire to live godly in Christ Jesus **will be** persecuted" (2 Timothy 3:12).*

Gut Check
Small Group Exercise

What is one takeaway myth about courage from this his chapter?

Which myth resonates the most with you and why?

Discuss C.S. Lewis' quote that, "Courage is not simply one of the virtues but the form of every virtue at the testing point, which means at the point of highest reality."

Read 2 Timothy 3:12. What did John Steinbeck mean when he wrote, "An unbelieved truth can hurt a man much more than a lie.

It takes great **courage** to back truth unacceptable to our times. There's a punishment for it, and it's usually crucifixion"?

CHAPTER 4

COURAGE: FOUR IRREFUTABLE ATTRIBUTES

"Nothing great will ever be achieved without great men, and men are great only if they are determined to be so. For glory gives herself only to those who have always dreamed of her."
—Charles De Gaulle (1890–1970)

"No great man lives in vain. The history of the world is but the biography of great men."
—Thomas Carlyle (1795–1881)

"It is not the strength of the body that counts, but the strength of the spirit."
—J.R.R. Tolkien (1892–1973)

*He said, "O man of high esteem, do not be afraid. Peace be with you; **take courage** and **be courageous**!" Now as soon as he spoke to me, I received strength and said, "May my lord speak, for you have strengthened me."*
Daniel 10:19

GEORGE WASHINGTON CARVER (1860-1943) WAS an American agricultural scientist and inventor who promoted alternative crops to cotton such as peanuts and sweet potatoes. He was arguably the most prominent black scientist of the early 20th century. While a professor at Tuskegee Institute, he developed techniques to improve soils depleted by repeated plantings of cotton.

But Carver **really** loved peanuts.

During his lifetime he developed 105 products using peanuts, but peanut butter was not one of them even though he is often credited for it. Probably thinking of those peanuts that he loved so much Carver once claimed, "Anything will give up its secrets if you love it enough."

Men love courage. We think about it. Just as little girls dream of their wedding day, little boys dream of the day they will be heroic. Men are drawn to courage much more than our lovely female counterparts. The movies we watch, books we read, and stories we tell all point to the fact that men are **obsessed** with courage. When they interact, courage is at the center of it all. We long for it. We live for it. We dream about the day we will be known for it. We live our lives trying to answer the elusive question, "Do I have what it takes?"

On the other hand, what books do women purchase, movies do they watch, and things do they discuss most often? Generally, women long for different things: love, security, deep relationships, and safe children. Men long for adventure, risk, and heroism.

All this to say that for more than two decades I have been obsessed with courage. I have studied it, watched movies about it, read books on the subject, and interviewed hundreds of courageous men for any secret that I might have missed. Courage inspires me. Witnessing courageous acts brings me to tears like nothing else.

In the previous chapter we exposed some misconceptions about courage that Christians inadvertently embrace.

In my exhaustive word study of courage over the past two decades I have discovered some tremendous secrets that were mined from the Bible. In this book, I offer them to you. It takes great courage to live out your best version. Cowards are never at their best. Only the courageous live freely, love boldly, and long to be their best in Jesus. Weak cowards need not apply.

Of the 57 times **courage**, or derivatives thereof, is mentioned in the Bible (NASB and NIV) it falls into one of four definitive categories. The discovery of these was life-changing in comparison to the three misconceptions we so often live by. Daniel 10:19 (below) is the only time two of these irrefutable attributes are listed together in the same passage; *"O man of high esteem, do not be afraid. Peace be with you; **take** courage and **be** courageous!"*

Here we see courage as both a character trait, "be courageous" and a personal choice, "take courage." Except for the Daniel 10:19 passage, every other time the Bible speaks of courage, it falls into one of the four attributes in this book. Let's briefly examine each of those four attributes that fill the guts of this book.

Courage is a call to action. It is interesting how many times the Bible mentions men losing, finding, gathering, and melting courage in the face of adversity. I almost named this attribute "Courage in the face of opposition" before realizing it is something much bigger.

Courage is a brutal call to action.

Courage almost always precedes calls to action in Scripture.

Why?

Because courage is not required to lounge on the couch, defer your fathering to another man, watch football while you family goes to church, or collect an unemployment check.

Edmund Burke (1729–1797) once said, "Evil prevails when good men do **nothing**." I would question how he meant the word "good" as it sounds synonymous with cowardly.

My friend Paul Coughlin who wrote the men's classic, *No More Christian Nice Guy*, might change Burke's meaning to, "Evil prevails when nice guys do nothing."

The bottom line is this: courage is needless for those who sit back and do nothing. It is, however, required to work your ass off for your family, confront the evils of this world, and fight for the souls of those you love. Courage is a requirement for those willing to act on their convictions and confront the bullies of this world.

Courage is a personal choice. A Holman "Thinline" New American Standard Bible (NASB) has been my personal study Bible since 1989. The spine is torn, pages that aren't ripped are stained, and decades of notes are faded into its pages. During my first exhaustive word study, I found 47 direct references to courage. Of those, 16 were commands to "take" courage. This blew me away. It was the first time I realized courage was a personal choice. People are brave because they choose to be.

Period.

Courage is an action. Courage is only a noun, a character trait, **after** the fact. When people are referred to as men of courage it is because they have a history of choosing courage time after time.

Fear is only a feeling. Fear, however, is the feeling that courageous men override to act valorously. When fear tempts us to shrink back (Hebrews 10:39), courage chooses to press on. It's simple. And profoundly difficult at the same time. How many men live as Ralph Waldo Emerson said, "Quiet lives of desperation," simply because they have chosen to embrace their fears and reject courage? How many choose wealth and comfort over significance and honor?

Courage is a sign of strength. Lastly, and probably the most obvious of the four irrefutable attributes is that courage is a sign of strength. I was working out with Shanna a while back and we usually do high intensity interval training (HIIT) workouts but on this occasion, we were bench pressing.

This a good time to explain a birth defect I've been cursed with. Without going into great detail for my mother's sake, most babies are born with their head larger than their chest. Not me. My chest and shoulders were **actually larger** than my head. Plus, I was a whopping 8 pounds, 12 ounces. As my mother retells on each birthday, "Jimmy (my mom still calls me Jimmy) it was like giving birth to twins!"

I grew up extremely self-conscious of my unusually large chest. I refused to take my shirt off in high school. But that chest earned me a full ride football scholarship. Back to the first story. I don't bench much. I don't need to. On this day, after not benching in months, I had 225 pounds on (I was over 50 at the time) and was repping it for sets of twelve when my wife, sensing my ego inflation, sneered, "No one cares how much you bench!"

No sooner had the words come out of her mouth when the local twenty-something Marine recruiter and his buddy walked over. "Wow, how much do you bench man! I wish I could push weight around like that!"

Don't make fun of my birth defect.

Men respect strength in all its various forms. Whether is it physical, mental, or spiritual. Men respect strength. They always have and always will. Men do not long to be courageous for courage's sake, but because they long to be seen as strong, capable, enduring men who defeat attrition in the face of adversity.

Courage is simply a means to an end. Men who are seen as strong are characterized as men of courage. The two, strength and courage, are two sides of the same coin. Where courage is lacking there is weakness. A man is strongest where he lives the most courageously. A Navy SEAL, for example is a man of strength and courage on the battle front but with astronomical divorce rates (90% during peace time)—is soft when it comes to marriage.

I was impressed to discover that of the 47 times that courage is mentioned in the Bible (NASB), 19 of those references are linked directly with strength.

· · ·

Nineteen times!

We simply cannot separate strength from courage in Scripture and will make no attempt in this book to do so.

Courage is a character trait. Looking at Daniel 10:19 reveals another irrefutable attribute of courage: be courageous. I believe that God places a deep desire to be courageous in the soul of every man. It's the elephant in the living room of his life. Do I have what it takes? Will I rise to the occasion? Am I good enough? Am I tough enough? Am I courageous?

Benjamin Disraeli once said, "Success is for a man to be ready for his time, when it comes." As stated earlier, courage as a character trait is attributed *after the fact*—after a man's *history* of making courageous decisions. The same is true for the coward. Cowardice is as cowardice does, just as courage is as courage does.

The male who defers the fathering of his children to another man is still a boy and a coward; not because he chooses it today, but because he has chosen it every day leading up to today. It is only when he chooses to act with courage that he starts the journey to courage.

Gut Check
Small Group Exercise

Why is Edmund Burke's statement "Evil prevails when good men do nothing" so important for us today?

Where have men gone silent?

Discuss each of the four irrefutable attributes of courage and what they mean to you.

Courage is a call to action.

Courage is a personal choice.

Courage is a sign of strength.

Courage is a character trait compounded over time.

Which of these is a growth area for you?

PART I. COURAGE, A CALL TO ACTION

CHAPTER 5

SEEING COURAGE

"All great and honorable actions are accompanied with great difficulties, and both must be enterprised and overcome with answerable **courage**."
—William Bradford (1590–1657)

Act with courage, and may the Lord be with those who do well.
2 Chronicles 19:11b NIV

"The bravest sight in the world is to see a great man struggling against adversity."
—Seneca (4 BC–65 AD)

*When they **saw the courage** of Peter and John and realized that they were unschooled, ordinary men, they were astonished and they took note that these men had been with Jesus.*
Acts 4:13

YEARS AGO, A MAN RESPONDED TO MY FAITH story with: "My mom was very sick when she was pregnant with me and I was supposed to be born handicapped or worse, but through the prayers of godly grandparents I am healthy and normal. I know I'm a miracle. I agree with you about Jesus, and who he is but I don't want to stop living my life."

Fear held him in bondage. The subtle fear of the unknown was elusive even to himself. His fear was subconscious to him, but it was fear, nonetheless. He was afraid of what he might become after Jesus deconstructed his life and put it back together again. Maybe he witnessed how God wrecked my life decades earlier and he wasn't willing to pay that great a price.

As Seneca observed in the First Century, "He who is brave is free."

This man believed following Jesus would make him **less** of a man. Sadly, his view of Christianity was skewed— or should I say screwed—by the effeminate stereotype of Jesus in the western Church.

What this man failed to recognize is that he remained only a shell of the version God created him to be. He is less of a man without Jesus—astronomically less. Jesus makes men better, stronger, more willing to heroically sacrifice himself in a valiant imitation of his Master who did the same for him (1 Peter 3:18).

This man's failed church experience clouded the truth that trusting God could make him **more of a man**, not less. A man will never summit the apex of masculinity without Christ. During a lifetime he may summit many other mountains of success, but the truth apex of masculinity is found only in Jesus, The Messiah. Reaching your full capacity can only be achieved by radical devotion to Him.

You may disagree. That's okay. You're still wrong. Look at it from this angle. If you believe there is a God, which most people do, then didn't He make you? If he made you, then doesn't He love you since you are one of His creations? If He made you, and loves you, then doesn't He know more about you than anyone else in the Universe—including you? If He made you, loves you, and knows you, then wouldn't He have a purpose for your existence? Would a loving creator make something with no purpose? Of course not! If God made you, loves you, knows you, and has a purpose for you, then how do you reach that purpose most effectively?

Simple. By radically pursuing the One who created you, loves you, knows you and has a purpose for you.

Anything else is like trying to summit a mountain on a moonless night after your headlamp batteries died. Good luck! How will a man ever achieve his God-given best version without radical devotion to the author of his life? Who will guide him there except the **only One** who knows what it is—his Creator?

In Acts 4 Peter and John were arrested after preaching the gospel and stand before "the rulers and elders and scribes" (Acts 4:5). After making their eloquent defense and preaching the gospel (Acts 4:8-12) to the very men who arrested them for doing so, the Jewish leaders made a profound discovery.

A few days back these were the same cowards who denied Jesus, ditched him in the Garden of Gethsemane, and hid. Now they're boldly proclaiming the gospel without fear or hesitation? What happened?

The Resurrection happened. Next, the Holy Spirit happened.

*"When they **saw the courage** of Peter and John and realized that they were unschooled, ordinary men, they were astonished, and they took note that these men had been with Jesus" (Acts 4:13).*

Courage is utilitarian. It rises out of ugliness. It grows from the fecal matter of human suffering. It is seen more than heard. Courage is function over form. If it can't be witnessed, then is probably isn't courage. Courage isn't found in macho vernacular, false bravado, or empty threats. It's found in results, action, and responsibility.

Only God makes ordinary men extraordinary. Any man who is not radically devoted to Jesus Christ is less than who he can be. It's that simple. It's that true even though billions of men who do not follow Jesus would vehemently disagree.

But they are still wrong and will find out just how wrong they are on The Day (Philippians 2:8-12).

Your best version was best described by Jesus in Matthew 6:33*: "But seek first His kingdom and His righteousness, and all these things will be given to you as well."*

Gut Check
Small Group Exercise

What was your biggest fear when you gave your life to Christ?

How did Jesus deconstruct your life?

What were the circumstances surrounding your salvation experience?

How is your life better now?

Read Acts 4:1-31. What truths do you see about courage?

List all the groups of people who were impacted by Peter and John's courage.

2 Chronicles 19:11b (NIV) says, *"Act with courage, and may the Lord be with those who do well."* The New American Standard Bible (NASB) translates it as, *"Act resolutely, and the Lord be with the upright."* What does it mean?

In Matthew 6:33 Jesus said, "But seek first His kingdom and His righteousness, and all these things will be given to you as well." Is it really that simple?

If so, what does prioritizing His kingdom and righteousness look like?

Chapter 6

Sufficient Courage

"Do not trust a warrior who cannot cry."
—Irish Proverb

*Most of the brethren, trusting in the Lord because of my imprisonment, have far more **courage to speak** the word of God without fear.*
Philippians 1:14

"The ultimate measure of a man is not where he stands in moments of comfort and convenience, but where he stands at times of challenge and controversy."
—Martin Luther King Jr. (1929–1968)

*I eagerly expect and hope that I will in no way be ashamed, but will have **sufficient courage** so that now as always. Christ will be exalted in my body, whether by life or by death.*
Philippians 1:20 NIV

WE WERE UP TO OUR CHESTS IN MUD, PUSHING AN empty duck boat to the ramp, which was nothing more than a sandy cutaway near Baywood Park. A group of bird watchers and, based on their laughter, anti-hunters watched the three of us struggle through the muck and shame, victims of one of Morro Bay's infamous minus tides.

We never even shot a duck.

Three 230-plus-pound men pushing a boat through the mud was quite a sight! One I would like to forget if it weren't for the opportunity to share it with you. Our story reminds me of the Apostle Paul who had an *"earnest expectation and hope" (Philippians 1:20 NASB)* that God would deliver him. Paul knew beyond the shadow of a doubt that God would pull him through life's muddy struggles.

So often men try to pull themselves through the mud. When we default to our own strength, we begin to trust the man in the mirror more than the God who made him. We think, "I'm tough. I've been here before. I can and will handle it." In those moments, which are more common than most of us want to admit, we still believe in Jesus, but momentarily trust in ourselves. We seek Christ but place our hope in our own strength *(Zechariah 4:6)*. In those moments we may claim to believe in Jesus but are little more than functional atheists.

Someone once said, "The problem with the self-made man is that he worships his creator." I couldn't agree more.

Eventually, however, we grow weary. It is hard being on the throne. Life is hard. Its propensity is to wear us down trudging through the muck and mire. When our faith is nothing more than functional atheism based on some erroneous "I'm a good person" theology, it's easy to lose sight of our true sustenance.

None of us are getting out of this life alive (until Christ that is). An elder statesman friend recently shared that, "Retirement is what you do in between doctor visits."

I ran into another friend, a man in his mid-eighties, who joked that, "At 82 everything on my body hurts, and the parts that don't hurt—don't work!"

Thanks for the heads up, man!

Our strength isn't enough. We must rely on Someone greater. We're all dying (2 Corinthians 4:16). Alone, our courage isn't enough, but God is the difference maker. Trusting Him is the edge needed to have sufficient courage to cross over from this life to the next. Do you trust Him today? Does your life bear witness against yourself that you are little more than a functional atheist?

Gut Check
Small Group Exercise

What is a functional atheist and how do you know if you are one or have backslidden into the state of functional atheism?

Share a story about a time you were stuck in the mud. What did you learn about yourself?

About God?

What is the difference between a functional atheist who claims he is a "Christian" and a Spirit-filled follower of Jesus?

Compare Philippians 1:20 in the New American Standard Bible (NASB) with that of the New International Version (NIV). What do you see?

What is your perspective on death and dying from 2 Corinthians 4:16-18?

If you were to die tomorrow, and stand before God, what would you say to prove that you were a devoted follower of Jesus on earth?

CHAPTER 7

FAILING COURAGE

"I have learned that success is to be measured not so much by the position that one has reached in life as by the obstacles which he has had to overcome while trying to succeed."
—Booker T. Washington (1856–1915)

They mounted up to the heavens
and went down to the depths;
*in their peril their **courage melted** away.*
Psalm 107:26 NIV

"If you're going through hell, keep going."
—Winston Churchill (1874–1965)

When we heard of it, our hearts melted and everyone's
***courage failed** because of you, for the Lord your God is God*
in heaven above and on the earth below.
Joshua 2:11

I LOVE FOOTBALL. I PLAYED IT THROUGH COLLEGE. I coached on every level from 3rd grade to high school varsity head coach. I write this as Linfield University's football chaplain. In all my years of playing, coaching, and watching football, one thing baffles me. I've never understood why football coaches use a Prevent defense in the final moments of a game. Can someone please help me understand the rationale behind such a reckless decision?

For those who don't know, the Prevent defense adds at least one more defensive back, drops Linebackers into coverage, removing at least two pass rushers in order to have more guys in coverage.

The argument for the Prevent is to strategically adjust to the overwhelming possibility that the offense **will** pass the ball. Adding more defenders in coverage, theoretically, limits the passing lanes.

But this strategy ignores two major football principles. First, it is true that with fewer pass rushers the quarterback has fewer open receivers. The flaw in this thinking, however, is that the quarterback has much more time to find an open receiver. It's a tactical tradeoff. I get it.

Second, the Prevent is a psychological move **away from** the original game plan in order to **prevent** defeat—to not lose. It hinders the defense from pinning its ears back and doing what got it there in the first place. The rule of the Prevent is to bend but not break, which is contrary to the overall defensive strategy to wreak havoc on an offense and break their will to win. This try-not-to-lose strategy changes the mindset of an otherwise aggressive system and, in my limited opinion, was a risk I was never willing to make.

The Prevent never existed in any of my defensive playbooks.

In my experience, all the Prevent does is prevent teams from winning. The bend-but-not-break strategy is soft, weak, and counterproductive. It is when coaches concede to a "melting" (Joshua 2.11) or "failing" (Psalm 107:26) of courage. Again, in my humble opinion, it's the beginning of the end and only a matter of time before a team concedes to defeat.

If you want to lose at anything in life the recipe is simple, focus on not losing and you will lose every time. We hit the target we have, even if we are seeking to avoid it.

In Joshua 2:11(above), Rahab's (the prostitute) alliance with the spies is motivated by the fear of what God had done so far. She knew the recent history. She remembered the Red Sea story. She heard the rumors. She saw the fear in her people.

Jericho lost the battle before it began. They knew it. The Israelites knew it. Rahab knew it, and did something about it, and she is famously recorded in the genealogy of Jesus (Matthew 1:5) and Faith Hall of Fame (Hebrews 11:31) for it.

History can be intimidating. All things being equal, a winning program has the upper hand over a losing one based only on winning tradition. Overcoming a history of failure is often the greatest struggle in building a winning life. Memories of failure can create an attitude of caution instead of reckless abandon—a Prevent defense—that ultimately hinders the **pin-your-ears-back** pursuit of victory.

. . .

Caution is the gateway to fear. It's a subtle yet highly effective way to ruin your life. I wonder if Ralph Waldo Emerson was thinking about the cautious life when he observed, "The mass of men leads lives of quiet desperation."

But winners hold the trophy before they've won it. They stick with the plan. Play to win. Pin their ears back. Go for it. Winners don't wade into icy waters. They jump.

Remember your history. It's a fact. You can't change it. Live in the present. Dream of your future. Rewrite yourself, and with God's help alter your legacy. When a man gets it—everyone wins.

Repent of trying not to lose. Yell at the television when teams revert to the Prevent, remembering what you read today. I do. Focus on the win. Focus on the prize (Philippians 3:12-16). Forge your future with reckless abandon.

May you live every day of your life.

Gut Check
Small Group Exercise

How has caution deceived you into a life of quiet desperation?

Where do you need to throw caution to the wind?

What risks do you need to take before the opportunity slips away?

Read the story of Rahab in Joshua 2:1-14. What do you notice about how some play to win while others play not to lose?

What does "failing" courage look like?

How do you recognize it?

What is the biblical response to it?

If you were one of the spies who met her, what kind of woman do you think she was?

What else can we gather about Rahab's life from Matthew 1:5, Hebrews 11:31, and James 2:25?

CHAPTER 8

REVERENT COURAGE

"People striving, being knocked down and coming back...
this is what builds character in a man."
—Tom Landry (1924–2000)

*Consider now, for the Lord has chosen you to build a house
for the sanctuary; be* **courageous and act***.*
1 Chronicles 28:10

"You become strong by defying defeat and by turning loss
and failure into success."
—Napoleon Bonaparte (1769–1821)

*He gave them these orders: "You must serve faithfully and
wholeheartedly in the* **fear** *of the Lord...* **act with courage***,
and may the Lord be with those who do well.*
2 Chronicles 19:9 & 11 NIV

What events eventually brought you to, or back to, Jesus? I was clueless about Christianity when I came to Christ, but eventually figured it out…kind of. God was trying to get my attention. In His great love for me, He saw that my path was leading me to a dark place that only pain could prevent.

God intervened with a fury that altered my life.

It started with a "routine" knee surgery that ended with anaphylactic shock after I was overdosed by the anesthesiologist. In one traumatic moment that is still a fog, I nearly went code blue, was blind three days due to severe eye swelling, and heard the voice of God for the first time while laying blind in the ICU. It was a call to ministry. A few months later I had reconstructive knee surgery while under a local anesthetic.

That was interesting!

Rehab was a small nightmare as I pushed to regain my former glory, but it was a futile attempt. During football Double Days I pulled several muscles in my good leg, which was still ten inches larger in circumference than my reconstructed leg. Midway through the season I spent four weeks in a hinge cast with a dislocated elbow. Then, a month later, I received a hairline fracture of the fibula.

Season over.

During my junior season, a near paralyzing neck injury ended my season after game five. It should have ended my career but against doctor's strong recommendations, I made the proverbial deal with God, had a great senior season, and surrendered my life fully to Him a few weeks later.

. . .

Men can be so stubborn.

To this day I search for God during pain. I always find Him there, unusually close when I am hurting. Not because He wants to hurt me but because He loves me enough to use pain to get my stubborn attention.

God uses pain to get our attention (Romans 8:28). We should be aware of God's **extreme** love for His children that goes to no ends to get our attention. God will go to extreme measures to bring us back to Him (1 Peter 3:18).

The Apostle Paul understood being blinded by God in order to see Him clearly. He understood the consequences of sin and would forever carry the thorn in his flesh (2 Corinthians 12:7) of near blindness (Galatians 6:11).

In Philippians 2:12 he warned believers, *"Continue to work out your salvation with fear and trembling."* To love God is to fear Him on some level. Be careful not to take 1 John 4:8 out of context, *"There is no fear in love; but perfect love casts out fear, because fear involves punishment, and the one who fears is not perfected in love."*

Know who you are. Know who God is. Know your role in the relationship with the Creator of the Universe. Do not fear condemnation (Romans 8:1), but the revelation of who He is and what He has done.

Never mistakenly ignore or neglect the jealous side of God *(Exodus 20:5)*. In 2 Chronicles 19:7-9 Jehoshaphat commissions his judges to rule the land, and *"fear the Lord."*

When raising our sons, we **demanded** obedience, with the promise of discipline. That discipline usually hurt. Fear raises Junior off the couch to take out the trash. Fear can be a motivator to act. As our children grow, the goal is that their obedience to us is not based on fear or "because I said so," but on a trusting relationship. Now the goal is for our adult children to follow **our** legacy because they love us and have determined ours is the right way to go.

Fear is not a bad thing. Fear motivates. Fear is a call to action. Fear is the conduit to acts of valor. Fear is a reverent understanding of God's nature. In Jesus, I don't fear God's wrath. I do, however, greatly fear disappointing Him. The "Parable of the Talents" in Matthew 25:14-30 is a great starting point if you disagree.

I fear what I see in Scripture and what I read is coming. To hide behind a single verse in the Bible (1 John 4:18) is theologically bad form, ignorant biblically, and leads to false teaching about God's character and nature.

It's the same with our relationship with God. We often start out fearing what He's capable of, but that relationship **must** transition to one of love and trust for us to experience God's fullness.

Gut Check
Small Group Exercise

How is 1 John 4:18 misinterpreted and why is taking the whole Bible (hermeneutics) into account vital to our understanding of biblical truth and the character of God?

How do you interpret Philippians 2:9-13 (specifically verse 12) considering 1 John 4:18?

Is this a contraction?

How do you reconcile the two?

Read the "Parable of the Talents" in Matthew 25:14-30. Where do you see reverent fear as a courage motivator?

In Matthew 25, how did fear (25) paralyze the "wicked and lazy (26)" servant?

Where has fear paralyzed you?

Where has fear prevented you for being at your best?

What fears have caused you great regret?

CHAPTER 9

MELTING COURAGE

"The world breaks everyone, and afterward, some are strong at the broken places."
—Ernest Hemingway (1899–1961)

*Their hearts **melted** and they no longer had the **courage** to face the Israelites.*
Joshua 5:1

"Victory belongs to the most persevering."
—Napoleon Bonaparte (1769–1821)

*When we heard it, our **hearts melted** and **no courage** remained in any man any longer because of you; for the Lord your God, He is God in heaven above and on earth beneath.*
Joshua 2:11 NIV

ONE FACT MANY PEOPLE DON'T KNOW IS THAT I was the head varsity football coach of my alma mater for most of one season. It happened after the former coach resigned on the bus ride to our second game. We won that game, but the season fell apart after our star running back suffered a season ending knee injury.

We were shocked by the head coach's mysterious resignation. To this day, it's still a mystery whispered among alumni. We tried to salvage the season for the sake of the team to no avail. Adding insult to injury, we were state champs with a perfect 13-0 the year before and were moved up a division to compete with schools twice our enrollment.

We ended a miserable 2-7.

During game week, before playing the soon-to-be undefeated state champions, I witnessed the defeat in our players' eyes. They knew they couldn't beat the perennial powerhouse. Heck, I knew it! But we were going to play our hearts out, throw our punches, and see what happened. No Prevent defense here. As a young head coach, I decided to attack and address their obvious loss of spirit head on.

But we still lost—**bad.**

We taught on Joshua 2:11 a few pages earlier called, "Failing Courage." Now we will look at it from the perspective of the New International Version, *"Our **hearts melted** and **no courage** remained in any man any longer because of you; for the Lord your God, He is God in heaven above and on earth beneath."*

I found it interesting that the cities feared most by the spies in the first report (Numbers 13:24-33) were the same ones whose hearts melted in fear. It's amazing how new perspectives, water under the bridge, and fresh leadership can change things.

Under new leadership, **Joshua's** generation was categorically different. They repented of the cowardice and complaining spirit of their parents and in doing so broke a generational curse (Exodus 20:5).

They crossed into the Promised Land and claimed it for their own. The book of Joshua is the most encouraging book of the Old Testament. Finally! A book where God's people almost always (Chapter 7 is coming) trust God.

Joshua 2:11 reminds me of the scariest movie of my childhood. Pathetically, it was a children's movie! I had nightmares for months of a wicked witch, flying on her broom, black costume and hat, threatening, "I'll get you my pretty, and your little dog, too."

I was horrified when she met her end, screaming as she painfully suffered, "I'm melting. I'm melting." It took me years before I could watch *The Wizard of Oz* again.

True story.

When I think of melting, I hear her wicked voice sinking into the depths.

I'm also very aware of those things that cause my heart to melt and courage fade whether they are financial burdens, ministry frustrations, or living adversaries. When triggered by a melting fear there is one passage I keep in my hip pocket. It has gotten me through some rough moments when I wanted to throw in the towel, leave the ministry, and settle into a comfortable life.

In Matthew 11:28-30 Jesus waves us over and says, *"Come to Me, all who are weary and heavy-laden, and I will give you rest. Take My yoke upon you and learn from Me, for I am gentle and humble in heart, and you will find rest for your souls. For My yoke is easy and My burden is light."*

When I feel like an ice cream cone on a hot summer's day, I meditate on this verse and life comes back into perspective. What triggers fear in you? What tempts your heart to melt? What do you do about it?

Gut Check
Small Group Exercise

What are the signs of a melting heart?

How do you know when fear is melting your courage?

What do you do?

Read Matthew 11:28-30. What stands out the most to you?

What does it mean to "take my yoke upon you" mean?

How do you do it?

Where are you most tempted to carry the burden God wants you to surrender to Him?

Read 1 Peter 5:6-8. What are some takeaways you can trust when you are feeling insignificant?

How do you "Cast your cares" to Him?

CHAPTER 10

PERILOUS COURAGE

*For they did not have **courage** to question Him any longer about anything.*
Luke 20:40

"We are frail, we are fearfully and wonderfully made, forged in the fires of human passion choking on the fumes of selfish rage, and with these our hells and our heavens so few inches apart, we must be awfully small, and not as strong as we think we are."
—Rich Mullins (1955–1997)

*Those who go down to the sea in ships, who do business on great waters; They have seen the works of the Lord, and His wonders in the deep. For He spoke and raised up a stormy wind, which lifted up the waves of the sea. They rose up to the heavens, they went down to the depths; Their **soul melted away** in their **misery**.*
Psalm 107:23-26

I WAS REMINDED OF THE POWER OF GOD WHILE
on a fishing trip in Sitka, Alaska, with my Dad and brother.
Dad has battled seasickness his entire life, but his love for
fishing keeps him going out, chum and all. He survived the
first two days of our trip, but the waves grew rougher and
on the third day Dad almost fell overboard losing his
breakfast over the stern. My brother Tom grabbed his belt
seconds prior to a dip in the ice-cold Pacific Ocean.

But those waves were a small gesture of God's
capability: *"Mightier than the thunder of the great waters,
mightier than the breakers of the sea—
the Lord on high is mighty" (Psalm 94:3).*

Think about how mighty God is in nature. The bravest
of men will run for cover in the path of a tornado. The
strongest of men will dash from the leaping flames of a
wildfire. The most brilliant of men will be silenced in awe
of the galaxies. The most athletic of men will concede to
the depths of God's great oceans. The most ingenious of
men will surrender to gravitational pull falling from 30,000
feet in the air.

Our perspective of God changes when we compare
God's power to our inconceivable speck in creation. We are
so small. The late Rich Mullins said it best: "We are not as
strong as we think we are." We cower in fear, melt away in
despair, and shudder in panic, when faced with the reality
of a perilous God who is jealous for us (Exodus 20:5).
Courage, the **soul** of valor, is "melted away" when standing
before the Creator of the universe.

Without Jesus as mediator (1 Timothy 2:3-5) no man
can stand in the presence of God, only fall to his knees and
shudder in fear: *"So then, my beloved, just as you have*

always obeyed, not as in my presence only, but now much more in my absence, work out your salvation with fear and trembling" (Philippians 2:12).

Every knee—even believers—will bow (Philippians 2:9-10). This is a legitimate fear. It's the kind that melts human courage in the face of the Divine. True courage, then, comes to the man who has been melted away by the presence of God.

We've made God too safe, kind, and nice. God is good, but He's anything but safe. And the word nice is never mentioned in the Bible to describe God, or any man for that matter. When I gave my life to Christ, my safe plans of American Dream fulfillment were destroyed in the wake of God's reckless will. My life is anything but safe. In fact, when life starts to feel safe, I know God is getting ready to disrupt it again. God wrecked my life, and I couldn't be more grateful. Trusting God is worth it. God is good. But to **truly** trust Him is to allow Him to deconstruct your life and dreams and replace them with something much better —His. Anyone who tells you that salvation leads to a life of comfort, pleasure, and prosperity is a liar and a heretic. Do not trust that man. Historically the opposite is often true when we look beyond our mortgaged windows.

Embrace this great paradox. The safest place to be is in the hands of the most dangerous Being in the universe: *"Therefore humble yourselves under the mighty hand of God, that He may exalt you at the proper time, casting all your anxiety on Him, because He cares for you" (1 Peter 5:6-7).*

Gut Check
Small Group Exercise

Compare Psalm 107:23-26 (above) in the New American Standard Bible and New International Version.

Discuss your findings.

Search and listen to Rich Mullins song, "We Are Not as Strong as We Think We Are."

How do the lyrics speak to you?

What does Philippians 2:9-12 teach you about our perilous God?

Is your God more on the nice or dangerous side and why?

Where do you need God to disrupt your safe and comfortable life?

What word picture do you see in 1 Peter 5:6-7?

What does cupped in the hands of God look like to you?

Pray for God's holy disruption of your comfortable plans.

Chapter 11

Casting Courage

"Courage is not the absence of fear but the awareness that something else is more important."
—Stephen Covey (1932–2012)

Do not fear, for I am with you; Do not anxiously look about you, for I am your God. I will strengthen you, surely I will help you, surely I will uphold you with My righteous right hand.
Isaiah 41:10

"Remember, when life's path is steep, to keep your mind even."
—Horace (65–8 BC)

*Now when Ish-bosheth, Saul's son, heard that Abner had died in Hebron, he **lost courage**, and all Israel was disturbed.*
2 Samuel 4:1

Do you remember learning how to fish? Two important factors in fishing are how to tie a hook, then how to cast the bait. I cast my first lure when I was around four years old. Dad was serious about angling.

I can only imagine how many of dad's precious lures I lost learning how to cast as a young boy, because learning to cast was never the goal. Catching fish was. Knowing the risks involved, Dad taught me where the fish liked to hide, which was usually near downfall, dead brush, and rocky outcroppings. My attempts to cast as close as possible to these underwater fortresses cost my dad a lot of hard-earned money. Snagging Dad's gear on trees, rocks, or watching a lure fly helplessly through the air because I forgot to take my finger off the spool was a routine I'm not proud of.

I quickly learned that one of three things were usually to blame for a lost lure—the size of the fish, a frayed line, or yours truly. I lost **far more** lures as a boy than I caught fish. I got pretty good at blaming the "one that got away" while holding a frayed line dangling aimlessly in the wind, Dad muttering more obscenities under his breath than I care to remember—most of the time screaming them!

In 2 Samuel 4 (above) we read about a man who cast his courage at another man. Ish-Bosheth was the fourth son of King Saul and the last representative of his family to be king over Israel.

History teaches that courage can't be deferred but is often wrongly projected upon a strong leader's courage—in this case Abner. This is only a Band-Aid. Every person, no matter how good, will eventually disappoint us or die; usually or both. Even the greatest of men have flaws. Even the strongest of men die. Courage cast in the wrong direction is eventually lost.

After the great warrior Abner died, Ish-Bosheth "lost courage." But was there a problem? At the time, he was the king and positional leader of Israel. When a leader is dependent on the courage of another, his followers are eventually "disturbed" and disappointed: *"Where there is no vision, the people perish" (Proverbs 29:18a KJV).*

Ish-Bosheth learned the hard way that no man can carry the burden of leadership for him. It cost him his life, killed by his two commanders while taking a nap (2 Samuel 4:5-8). The Hebrew of 2 Samuel 4:1 for *"Lost courage"* literally means *"his hands dropped."* He made a bad cast, put down his pole, and stopped fishing.

His shoulders slumped in defeat. His head hung low. His spirit was broken.

Who do you entrust your courage to—yourself, your employer, the government? How about your family? Do cast your courage to your wife or church to take care of those you love?

Mistake.

In 2020 the Coronavirus pandemic created mass panic, protests, and turmoil as people's trust of the government to protect them imploded. The convergence of these (pandemic, presidential election, and race riots) is not a coincidence but the fruit of a people who do not trust God. Let 2020 be a lesson to us all, that a man's courage is only as strong as the one he trusts the most.

Where is your courage cast? How you handle adversity bears witness to who or what you trust the most. Ish-Bosheth's fatal mistake brings Peter's words to life: *"**Cast** *all your anxiety on him (Jesus) because he cares for you" (1 Peter 5:7).*

Like the hundreds of lures lost over the years, casting courage in the wrong direction ultimately breaks the line of faith. No man is worthy of **your** courage. No system is worthy of your implicit trust.

Trust in what will never fray or snap under resistance. Discover the power that comes from casting your courage upon the One who will never fail. The man who trusts in Him will not get snagged.

Gut Check
Small Group Exercise

Read about Ish-Bosheth's demise in 2 Samuel 4:1-8. What other mistakes do you see? Why did he trust in Abner to a fault?

Are you casting your trust anywhere you shouldn't?

Who are you mistakenly trusting?

Are you snagged because you have projected your courage away from Jesus?

What new insights have you gathered from 1 Peter 5:7? How does verse 8 add context to the severity of misplaced trust?

How is David's courage different from Saul's and Ish-Bosheth's?

CHAPTER 12

STIRRING COURAGE

"The two hardest tests on the spiritual road are the patience to wait for the right moment and the **courage** not to be disappointed with what we encounter."
—Paulo Coelho
Veronika Decides to Die

"**Courage** is like love; it must have hope for nourishment."
—Napoleon Bonaparte (1769–1821)

In a time of tranquility he will enter the richest parts of the realm, and he will accomplish what his fathers never did, nor his ancestors; he will distribute plunder, booty and possessions among them, and he will devise his schemes against strongholds, but only for a time.
Daniel 11:24

IF YOU'VE EVER MET A CONTRARIAN, YOU'LL KNOW
it. They love to argue. They enjoy ticking people off with
their Devil's Advocate attitude. They look at life through
different lenses. They live to contradict. They're
argumentative. They question everything for the sake of
the question

If I say it's white, they say it's black just because I said
white. They know how to get under people's skin and are
experts at doing it. If their opinions don't frustrate, they
may spur someone on *(Hebrews 10:24-25),* but more often
they make people want to kick their behind.

They would probably disagree with the "contrarian"
label, which the Bible identifies as "quarrelsome" (1
Timothy 3:3). But they disagree with almost everything
anyway, so who cares?! Interestingly, out of the twenty
qualifications of spiritual leadership mentioned in the
Pastoral Epistles—1 Timothy, 2 Timothy, and Titus—
being quarrelsome is a strike against the man who wants to
lead others spiritually.

I positively identify the non-quarrelsome person as a
"Peacemaker." In his classic *Measure of a Man*, Getz
explains, "Paul was concerned about the man who
habitually demonstrates inappropriate attitudes and
actions. He is also concerned about the unpredictable
person, the man who at times is congenial, and at times,
seemingly without provocation, stirs up argument and
throws a wrench in the spiritual machinery that God
designed to create peaceful relationships."

Without wading too deep into weeds, let's observe
Daniel 11 in staying true to our subject of courage. In verse
25 we learn that this mysterious future king of the North

"will stir up his strength and courage against the king of the South with a large army."

Becoming your best version of a man is the most difficult journey you will take, which is why we need a guide. The Bible is our greatest tool, but we all need men to teach us how to wield it, and lead us where we have never been, which is why our organization, Men in the Arena, exists.

A man's strength manifests in the size and quality of his army. In Mark 2:1-12 we read the memorable story about the paralyzed man who was healed after his buddies lifted his broken body above the crowd, tore the roof apart, and lowered their friend to Jesus's lap. I love what Mark records in verse 5, *"And when Jesus saw **their** faith, he said to the paralytic, 'Son, your sins are forgiven.'"*

Jesus saw beyond the roof debris to the faith of a few good men! The paralyzed man never speaks, and the only thing he brings to the story is his brokenness. His greatest asset was his personal army—the men on the roof who healed him through **their** faith.

A man's strength and wealth are measured by the size and quality of his army. The contrarian I described earlier separates himself from others. Thus, his army is small, weak, and soft regardless of wealth and superficial success. Though I'm sure he would disagree.

Muster your army. Raise an entourage of people who have your back.

It takes all types. We need different kinds of people in our life. We need contrarians who **call us out**. Men who push back even when you don't want to be pushed. The contrarian loves to ask questions that no one else asks. At times they are quarrelsome, bothersome, and annoying, but they serve a purpose if their heart is for you to win.

We need men who **call us in**. These men are committed at all costs. They will follow us into the darkest places. They don't shy away or shrink back from our lowest moments. They are men we can call at 2:00 in the morning. Men who have our back. They are like the, "friend who sticks closer than a brother" (Proverbs 18:24).

We need men who will **call us up**. They are guides, mentors, and models. They have been where we want to be. They see potential in us that we don't see in ourselves. They lead the way towards our best version.

Recruit men for your roof. Join a small group. Start building your army. Increase your strength. Enhance your courage. Reach your full capacity.

Gut Check
Small Group Exercise

Read about the healing of the paralytic and the men on the roof in Mark 2:1-12 and Luke 17-26. Look carefully at how many men were involved (Hint: it was not four).

How many do you think were there and what different roles did they place in his healing?

Look at Proverbs 27:17 and Hebrews 10:24-25. Who sharpens you?

Who calls you out, in, and up?

Who spurs you on and how do they do it?

What is Christian brotherhood?

How it is like a biological family?

Different?

Reflect on Proverbs 18:24. Who are your 2:00 in the morning friends and what do they say about you?

PART II - COURAGE: A PERSONAL CHOICE

CHAPTER 13

COURAGE: GATHER IT

"I wanted you to see what real **courage** is, instead of getting the idea that **courage** is a man with a gun in his hand. It's when you know you're licked before you begin, but you begin anyway and see it through no matter what."
—Atticus Finch
To Kill a Mockingbird

Because the hand of the Lord my God was on me, I took **courage and gathered** *leaders from Israel to go up with me.*
Ezra 7:28 NIV

Joseph of Arimathea came, a prominent member of the Council, who himself was waiting for the kingdom of God; and he **gathered up courage** *and went in before Pilate, and asked for the body of Jesus.*
Mark 15:43

I KNEW SNOWBOARDING WOULD NOT BE A HOBBY I would ever enjoy the day I was ice sliding down a mountain when two pink elementary school girls blurred by me with their matching outfits and blonde ponytails methodically dancing under their helmets as their dad yelled, "Girls watch out for that big guy!"

Of course, I did what any surprised ice slider would do when blinded by a pink flurry.

I crashed. A garage sale ensued. A "garage sale" is when your gear is aggressively separated from your body and slides all over the mountain. You then have the joyous opportunity to chase it, on foot, as it slides down the mountain.

People pay for this stuff? I am very aware of gathering things up, although I would much rather gather my duck decoys, shoot colorful limits, retrieve my arrows after shooting a minute-of-angle group at 100 yards, or hold Shanna's hand while driving.

Shanna should have known snowboarding could never compete with upland and waterfowl season, but I tip my hat to her for trying. Who would want to slide down a glacier on a board, when they can sit in waist deep water for six hours in leaky waders during a torrential rainstorm anyway?!

Mark 15:33-39 records the death of Jesus. Afraid for their lives, the disciples had ditched him, Peter had denied him, and John seems to be the only disciple to witness Jesus's death, most likely in disguise. The next three days would be spent hiding from the authorities in fear for their lives.

. . .

Then, out of nowhere, a hero appears—Joseph of Arimathea.

Matthew 27:57 describes him simply as a rich man and disciple of Jesus, but according to Mark he was "*a respected member of the council, who was also himself looking for the kingdom of God.*" Luke 23:50–56 adds that he, "*had not consented to their decision and action.*"

In other words, Joseph had a lot to lose by associating with Jesus—including his life.

We don't see him until after the crucifixion. Was he hiding? Clearly, he was deathly afraid, but he overcame his fear as "*he gathered up courage and **went** in before Pilate and asked for the body of Jesus.*"

He experienced fear, deep, almost paralyzing fear. But he mentally regrouped. He gathered up his scattered courage. He cleaned up the garage sale that fear had scattered, and he went.

He made a choice to override fear, acted, and is forever remembered for the courage of a single act.

Has your courage been scattered so long that it seems lost? Have you lost yourself somewhere along the way? If you've been separated from courage, maybe it's time to gather it back up. Claim it as your own.

And he went.

Gut Check
Small Group Exercise

Compare Ezra 7:28 (above) in the New International Version with other translations. What do you see?

What do you learn about courage?

Mark 15:43 says, "Joseph of Arimathea came, a prominent member of the Council, who himself was waiting for the kingdom of God; and he **gathered up courage** and went in before Pilate and asked for the body of Jesus."

What insight can you gather about Joseph?

What else do you know about Joseph of Arimathea from Matthew 27:57, Mark 15:43, and Luke 23:50–56?

What does he teach us about courage?

CHAPTER 14

COURAGE: TAKE IT

"Endurance is not just the ability to bear a hard thing, but to turn it into glory."
—William Barclay (1907–1978)

*"**Take courage** and be men, O Philistines, or you will become slaves to the Hebrews, as they have been slaves to you; therefore, be men and fight."*
1 Samuel 4:9

"It is doubtful whether God can bless a man greatly until He has hurt him deeply."
—A.W. Tozer (1897–1963)

*When Asa heard these words and the prophecy of Azariah son of Oded the prophet, he **took courage**.*
2 Chronicles 15:8

A friend walked into my office and said, "I don't know what this means, but God wants you to 'Take it.'"

That was it. He delivered his message and left. No explanation. No back story. He refused to offer any interpretation of those two words. He walked in, delivered the message and left. Don't shoot the messenger. I remember wondering, "Take what?" Three months later we were offered a job, took it, and moved to McMinnville, Oregon.

Remember, courage isn't a gift from God (1 Corinthians 12:1-29), a fruit of the Spirit (Galatians 5:22-23), or one of the Ten Commandments (Exodus 20:1-17). It has nothing to do with natural ability. Courage isn't a part of God's grand scheme of blessings. God doesn't give courage.

It may not be a fruit of the Spirit, but it is low hanging fruit for those bold enough to grab ahold of it. In the Bible, as in life, men **take** it.

God gives opportunities for courage, but someone has to reach out and **take it**. I was offered that job in McMinnville, but it meant nothing without **taking** it. The man that never takes courage remains a spoon-fed boy who refuses to grow up. Manhood demands it. Life requires it. The world needs it.

Hebrews 5:12-14 warns, *"Anyone who lives on milk, being still an infant, is not acquainted with the teaching about righteousness. But **solid food** is for the mature, who by constant use have trained themselves to distinguish good from evil."*

· · ·

You see, courage is a call to action and a choice. It's the solid food of masculinity. A man can wait on God for many things, but courage is not one of them. Courage is action. Action must be taken. When fear tempts him to flight or freeze, courage **frees** a man to fight for what he believes and those he loves. No one can be free except through courage.

Stop blaming God for your inability to act on what He's put on your heart (Psalm 40:1). And stop asking Hm to do what he has already asked you to do. Stop praying about what you know to be true and act. Just do it. There's no place in Scripture where God gives courage as some kind of gift. He offers it to men with the guts enough to **take it**.

Gut Check
Small Group Exercise

1 Samuel 4:9 (above) and 2 Chronicles 15:8 (above) call men to "take courage."

Where else in the Bible do you see this?

What is usually happening when men are called to "take courage?"

What is usually happening in your life when courage is required?

When you experience fear, are you most tempted to fight, flight, or freeze?

Explain.

What area is screaming for you to reach up and take courage?

CHAPTER 15

COURAGE: HOLD IT

"Be sure you put your feet in the right place, then stand firm."
—Abraham Lincoln (1809–1865)

"There are two great days in a person's life—the day we are born and the day we discover why."
—William Barclay (1907–1978)

*But Christ is faithful as a son over God's house. And we are his house, if we **hold** on to our **courage** and the hope of which we boast.*
Hebrews 3:6

Native hunters in the jungles of Africa have a clever way of trapping monkeys. They slice a coconut in two, hollow it out, and in one half of the shell cut a hole just big enough for a monkey's hand to pass through. Then they place an orange in the other coconut half before fastening together the two halves of the coconut shell. Finally, they secure the coconut to a tree with a rope, retreat into the jungle, and wait.

Sooner or later, an unsuspecting monkey swings by, smells the delicious orange, and discovers its location inside the coconut. The monkey then slips his hand through the small hole, grasps the orange, and tries to pull it through the hole. Of course, the orange won't come out; it's too big for the hole. To no avail the persistent monkey continues to pull and pull, never realizing the danger he is in.

While the monkey struggles with the orange, hunters either sneak in and capture the monkey by throwing a net over him, or kill it. If the monkey keeps his death grip on the orange, it is trapped. The longer a man is gripped by fear the more vulnerable he becomes.

I shared earlier, one of the most influential studies in my life was an exhaustive Bible study on "**courage**" that became this book. At that time in 2001, I sensed God leading to a place that would take great courage. What I didn't know was that a few months later, courage would be needed to move my young family from California to Oregon. A decade later we needed more courage to step out in faith and pioneer The Great Hunt for God, what you know as Men in the Arena.

The major takeaway from my time with Courage was this: **courage must be taken.** It isn't something you receive. It's not a fruit of the Spirit. It's not a spiritual gift. It's not a talent. **Courage must be taken** (1 Samuel 4:9).

Courage challenges our status quo.

Courage isn't a feeling either. It's often a response contrary to our feelings. Actually, courage is often birthed out of fear. The "feeling" we experience while acting courageously **is** fear. In other words, the feeling of fear usually accompanies a courageous act. I love the acrostic that fear is "false evidence appearing real." Men either rise to meet the challenge of their fears or fall into cowardice.

Courage acts. Cowardice surrenders.

Courage is the response of faith. When fear manifests, courage leans in a ruthless act of trust: *"Trust in the Lord with all your heart, and do not lean on our own understanding. In all your ways acknowledge Him, and He will direct your paths" (Proverbs 3:5-6).*

Unlike a spiritual gift, talent, or fruit of the Spirit, courage is one thing God asks men to choose—to take *(Psalm 31:24).*

But **taking** courage isn't enough. It isn't sustainable.

Once taken, it must be held onto. Today's Courageous men can be tomorrow's Cowards **if** they don't ferociously grip courage like a monkey holding on to an orange.

The more of the world we hold, the more difficult it is to keep our grip on courage, which often slips through our fingers. Hold on to it every day, all the time.

Hold courage. Never let it go *(Acts 23:11).*

Gut Check
Small Group Exercise

Philippians 2:15-16 (above) talks about "holding fast" to the Word of Life. Why is this so important in living with courage?

What does "hold on to our courage" look like (Hebrews 3:6)?

How does it manifest in your life?

"Trust in the Lord with all your heart, and do not lean on our own understanding. In all your ways acknowledge Him, and He will direct your paths" (Proverbs 3:5-6).

What is trust?

How is it different than cognitive assent?

How are trust and belief (Romans 10:9-10) similar?

Where do you need to strengthen your grip (Psalm 31:24)?

CHAPTER 16

COURAGE: KEEP IT

"The wise man in the storm prays to God, not for safety from danger, but for deliverance from fear."
—Ralph Waldo Emerson (1803–1882)

*Yet now I urge you to **keep up your courage**, for there will be no loss of life among you, but only of the ship."*
Acts 27:22

"If you can't fly, then run, if you can't run, then walk, if you can't walk, then crawl, but whatever you do, you have to keep moving."
—Martin Luther King Jr (1929–1968)

*Therefore, **keep up your courage**, men, for I believe God that it will turn out exactly as I have been told. But we must run aground on a certain island.*
Acts 27:25

On my first trip to Maui I went snorkeling and, to my amazement, could float in the saltwater with the best of them! However, remove the snorkel and mask, put me in fresh water, and I epitomize Bob Seger's song, *Like a Rock.*

I can swim, but it takes so much work to stay afloat, my body tires easily, and I begin to sink. I'm glad no one can see how much I must be sweating underwater.

Courage is like watching me try to swim. It takes a lot of work and constant attention. Without effort and proper body position, the propensity of **my** body is to sink.

Courage operates the same way. Courage lacks buoyancy without training, effort, and focus. It's work. It's a choice. It takes effort to **keep** courage **up**.

In *Acts 27*, Paul's ship is sinking and twice, in four verses, he admonishes the crewman to, *"Keep up your courage."* When fear begins to pull you under, fight to keep courage afloat. When your courage is tired from treading water without any forward progress, lean back, hold your head up and keep moving your arms.

It reminds me of the quote from Martin Luther King Jr.: "If you can't fly, then run, if you can't run, then walk, if you can't walk, then crawl, but whatever you do, you have to keep moving forward."

The good news when the storms of life throw you overboard is that life suddenly becomes simplified. Sink or swim. Float or drown. Live or die. If you can't stay on the boat, then swim, if you can't swim, then float, if you can't float, then tread water, if you can't tread water then scream, but whatever you do, you have to keep moving.

. . .

Courage takes work to stay buoyant. It takes movement. Courage is not static. A man may swim through the currents of life one day and drown in the undertow of apathy the next.

Courage is a fight.

Courage is a verb.

Courage must be kept buoyant.

When life's undertow begins to wear you down, tread water.

Move your arms. Identify the resistances in your life and begin swimming. It's there that you'll begin to keep your courage up.

Gut Check
Small Group Exercise

Ponder Martin Luther King Jr.'s quote, "If you can't fly, then run, if you can't run, then walk, if you can't walk, then crawl, but whatever you do, you have to keep moving forward."

How can you personalize it?

Read the story about Paul in the Mediterranean Sea storm in Acts 27:22-25.

How does the crew respond differently than Paul?

Why?

What did Paul know that they didn't?

What storm are you in right now?

What did the author of Hebrews mean when he wrote, "This hope we have as an **anchor** of the soul, a *hope* both sure and steadfast and one which enters within the veil" (Hebrews 6:17-19)?

CHAPTER 17

COURAGE: FIND IT

"I fear not the man who has practiced 10,000 kicks once, but I fear the man who has practiced one kick 10,000 times."
—Bruce Lee (1940–1973)

*For You, O my God, have revealed to Your servant that You will build for him a house; therefore Your servant has **found courage** to pray before You.*
1 Chronicles 12:25

"Fortitudine vincimus. Through endurance we conquer."
—Ernest H. Shackleton (1874–1922)
Family Motto

*For You, O Lord of hosts, the God of Israel, have made a revelation to Your servant, saying, "I will build you a house," therefore Your servant has **found courage** to pray this prayer to You.*
2 Samuel 7:27

Have you experienced a moment when your heart sank? When something hit you that you knew would change your life forever? A last second defeat? Being fired over something preventable? Saying something hurtful to a loved one that you can never take back? Missing the Highway Patrol as you sped by him?

One memorable elk hunt stands out. What I'm about to share wasn't pretty but it is the truth. After chasing off a smaller bull, which also would have been the biggest bull of my life, the herd bull strutted 30 yards in front of me screaming, pissing on himself, spinning in circles—a territorial dance that says, "If you mess with this bull again, you will get the horns." He was so aggressively making a statement to the lesser "Satellite" bull, that I was forced to hold at full draw for over a minute watching his circular war dance. He spun for what seemed like forever while the lesser bull repeatedly screamed over the recent loss of his ten now ex-girlfriends.

When the large bull we nicknamed the "Saber Bull" finally stopped broadside, I released the arrow. But something felt horribly wrong. I had inadvertently let off on the bow a half of an inch, causing the bow to lose power, the arrow missing its mark—a non-fatal shot. I just missed the easiest shot of my life!

Panic stricken at missing what should have been a slam dunk, elk fever may have been a slight actor, I quickly nocked a second arrow, knowing it would be my last, came to full draw, and let out a deep breath. By this time the bull was **hard** quartering away, at over forty yards, looking back for the strange bug that bit him in the chest. My easiest shot was now the toughest shot of my life as I held my 30-yard pin high, guessing the distance at over 40 yards.

I released arrow number two. In the dusk light I didn't see the flight of the arrow only the "smack" of solid contact. All Hell broke loose as the bull whirled around, headed for the tree line, as the darkness swallowed him.

All was silent. Eerie. Deathly calm. The phantom bull was gone. I distinctly remember the smell of Juniper was the only distinguishable sign of life.

A quick search found arrow number one, a few drops of blood, and pitch blackness lit only by my desperate head lamp. My hunting buddy, Philip went one way and I went the other in a desperate search for a missed opportunity. Several minutes later my buddy returned to tell me that he found a good blood trail and I needed to follow him quickly. He led me to the spot, pointed into the darkness, "Look, there's the pool of blood. Do you see it?"

Staring into the darkness, I saw it. Like a massive tree branch out of place in the sea of sage was a lone branch. It was an antler! Two hundred yards from shot number two, my bull was down, and in an instant, I went from mourning to celebration. I went from the outhouse to the penthouse! I know the exhilaration of having something slip through your fingers only to find it once again.

Have you experienced the joy of finding something you lost? I bet you can relate to the shepherd in Luke 15:6 who found his lost sheep: *"And when he comes home, he calls together his friends and his neighbors, saying to them, 'Rejoice with me, for I have found my sheep which was lost!'"*

Only a handful of the 57 times courage is recorded in Scripture do we see courage **lost** or **found**, but they are deeply significant, nonetheless. Courage is easily lost in the mundane routines of life. Like a bat in the dark, it vanishes into an overwhelming schedule, high demands of manhood, and the normal troubles of life.

In 2 Samuel 7:18-29 David, who was famous for his bravery, prayed a beautiful prayer: *"For You, O Lord of hosts, the God of Israel, have made a revelation to Your servant, saying, 'I will build you a house'; therefore Your servant has found courage to pray this prayer to You."*

David was to bravery what Solomon was to wisdom, and he teaches us a great lesson about it. Courage oscillates between feelings and truth, cowardice and valor, passivity and action. The only difference between them is that brave men act in spite of their fears. When they realize their courage is lost, they put on the headlamp, get close to the ground and search until it is found again.

Gut Check
Small Group Exercise

Read about the lost sheep, lost coin, and lost son in
Luke 15.

What extremes do the shepherd, woman, and father go to
so they can find the lost things they love?

Meditate on your life. Are there any areas that need you to
find courage?

What are they?

Fear is subtle and difficult to identify. Are there dreams
you've allowed to vanish into the dark that, if you are
honest, were motivated by fear?

Read the prayer of David in 2 Samuel 7:18-29. What truths
do you see about finding courage?

CHAPTER 18

COURAGE: FIGHT IT

"I have not failed. I've just found 10,000 ways that won't work."
—Thomas Edison (1847–1931)

Finally, be strong in the Lord and in the strength of His might. Put on the full armor of God, so that you will be able to stand firm against the schemes of the devil.
Ephesians 6:10-11

*Even if you go and **fight courageously** in battle, God will overthrow you before the enemy, for God has the power to help or to overthrow.*
2 Chronicles 25:8 NIV

AS A YOUNG AND AMBITIOUS YOUTH PASTOR I WAS once invited to speak to a local service club on the topic of "reaching teenagers in our community." Young and zealous, I delivered my best sermon on saving the lost souls of our small community in the name of Jesus.

But five minutes into my message, I noticed jaws dropped, fried egg eyes all over the room, and looks of shock. It hit me. This isn't a Christian gathering! This was a secular service club, and the message I was asked to give wasn't supposed to be a sermon!

Many of the men and women in the audience—most of them—were **the** lost souls I was talking about reaching for Christ! Apparently, I misinterpreted the word "reach!" I hate when that happens! A handful of affirming smiles from believers in the audience encouraged me to preach on.

So, I went for it.

It was too late anyway. I had already waded into deep waters. What were they thinking when asked a **pastor** to speak? We only know how to talk about one thing, Jesus. It's what we do. I thought to myself, "What the heck. I won't be asked back so I might as well go for it. What are they going to do, crucify me?!"

I pushed over the frowns and finished strong. Why is it that men equate Christianity to being passive and soft? Why would a secular service club think a pastor would back down from preaching the gospel (Hebrews 10:39)? Why is it that the more religious an Islamic man is, the more manly they are perceived? Why then, are the more religious Christian men expected to be somehow weaker and softer even though they model their lives after the manliest man in human history?

Famous preacher Charles H. Spurgeon once said, "There has got abroad a notion, somehow, that if you become a Christian, you must sink your manliness and turn milksop."

It simply is not true. In fact, it's the opposite. To follow Jesus is only for the strong and brave. Over the years, I've seen weak men fall by the wayside of faith, unwilling to bear the cross of Jesus, choosing the lesser—easier life of pleasure, comfort, and overindulgence.

Did you know the word fight is mentioned almost 200 times in the Bible? War is mentioned nearly 400 times and destroy over 500 times? The same God, the God who never changes (Hebrews 13:8) still sits on the throne. Am I telling you to pick a fight with someone? Yes, I am.

Like William Wallace's character in the movie, *Braveheart* when asked what he is about to say to the English king, he simply smiled and said, "I'm going to pick a fight."

I'm telling you to pick a fight with your lesser version. Declare war on your weaker self. Make choices against yourself. Climb out of the arena floor, up the stadium stairs, into the anonymous bleachers, grab your cowardly self and beat the fear out of that guy until the only thing that remains is courage. Do you want to be brave? Do you want to be a man of courage? You had better be willing to fight your lesser self for it.

Gut Check
Small Group Exercise

Read about the story of King Amaziah in 2 Chronicles 25, especially verse 8. Where does Amaziah exhibit great courage?

What is his source and how can you imitate him?

Why do we so often ignore all the references to fighting, war, and destruction in the Bible only to engage of the heresy of false Christology through a lopsided view of grace?

Look at Jesus's destruction of the temple in John 2:13-25?

Discuss what this scene would have looked like?

What emotions do you see in Jesus?

The vendors?

The religious leaders?

How do Mark 3:1-5 and 10:13-15 send a message to those who think Jesus was always calm, soft, and polite?

Where is your view of Jesus skewed and need of a theological adjustment?

CHAPTER 19

COURAGE: STRENGTHEN IT

*That is why, for Christ's sake, I delight in weaknesses, in insults, in hardships, in persecutions, in difficulties. For when I am weak, then I am **strong**.*
2 Corinthians 12:9-10

"Many men owe the grandeur of their lives to their tremendous difficulties."
—Charles Spurgeon (1834–1892)

*I was **strengthened** according to the hand of the Lord my God upon me, and I gathered leading men from Israel to go up with me.*
Ezra 7:28b

*Because the hand of the Lord my God was on me, I **took courage** and gathered leading men from Israel to go up with me.*
Ezra 7:28b NIV

I REFUSE TO SING CERTAIN SONGS IN CHURCH. IF they're untrue or too effeminate, I choose silence. For example, take these lyrics from a popular worship song, *"Great is your love and justice God. You use the weak to lead the strong."*

What? Did you read that? Think about this statement biblically, now practically? We **sing** this in churches as if it were true?

It isn't true! It's false teaching. It's not true in the Bible or human history. It never will be.

Why this song reached such wild popularity speaks to the decline of masculinity and biblical knowledge in the American Church.

When do the weak **ever** lead the strong in Scripture? Show me one reference in context. My best guess is that this atrocity of a worship song is a gross misinterpretation of 2 Corinthians 12:9-10: *"'My grace is sufficient for you, for my power is made perfect in weakness.' Therefore I will boast all the more gladly about my weaknesses, so that Christ's power may rest on me. That is why, for Christ's sake, I delight in weaknesses, in insults, in hardships, in persecutions, in difficulties. For **when I am weak, then I am strong**."*

If my guess is true, contextually speaking, the song is way off mark. The passage offers no reference to leadership in the midst of weakness.

Maybe, you argue, he's thinking about Gideon. In Gideon's case we see God turn a man who saw himself as **weak** into a mighty warrior (Judges 6). Let me explain my point before you throw rocks at your worship leader. I wholeheartedly—enthusiastically—agree that God makes weak people stronger. Gideon started weak but didn't stay that way. God changed him. God does that.

The disciples were weak in many ways. Joseph was the youngest, therefore weakest of the 12 brothers. Jacob was physically weaker than Esau.

The weak don't lead the strong in Scripture until they become strong. Even fictional movie characters never follow the weak. Never. No one does. It never happens. How men in churches blindly sing heretical songs without flinching is beyond me.

We have been blinded by the enemy.

These are the blind guides Jesus warned us about in Matthew 15:14: *"Let them alone; they are blind guides of the blind. And if a blind man guides a blind man, both will fall into a pit."*

Leaders are strong. They are courageous. Any man can be transformed from weak (I am not talking about physically) to strong. I see men who are small in stature lead larger men all the time. Stature does not make a man strong, courage does. Romans 12:2 says it best: *"Do not conform to the pattern of this world, but be transformed by the renewing of your mind. Then you will be able to test and approve what God's will is—his good, pleasing and perfect will."*

Courage is forged through the truth of God's word, not some feeling or lyric that rhymes well. Strong men don't follow weak men. They never will. Like William Wallace's character in the movie, *Braveheart*: "People don't follow titles. They follow courage."

Yes, God uses the foolish things of the world to shame the wise *(1 Corinthians 1:18-25)*, but we can't bridge the gap between foolishness and weakness in Scripture. I think of Joshua, Gideon, Solomon, Jacob, Joseph, and many others who may have started weak by human standards, until they were strengthened by Yahweh.

God's Word is the compass to finding true strength. Be discerning about the **effeminate** voices in the modern Church unintentionally detouring men from their best version in Him. Strive to know the Word better than your pastor, worship leader, and anyone in your family. Tap into its power. Tap into its strength. Lead well my brothers.

Gut Check
Small Group Exercise

Think about your church. What heretical songs or false teachings have you ignored because of fear, indifference, or ignorance?

Why has this become such a problem in Churches today?

Why are Christian men so often seen as weaker?

Read 2 Corinthians 12:9-10 in context. How do you interpret it?

In Philippians 4:12-13 Paul boasted that he could do all things through Christ who strengthened him. What did he mean?

How do you interpret "all things?"

Compare Ezra 7:28 in the New American Standard Bible (NASB), New International Version (NIV) and other translations.

Why are strength and courage so closely linked?

CHAPTER 20

COURAGE: DO IT

"One man with courage is a majority."
—Thomas Jefferson (1743–1826)

*But prove yourselves **doers** of the word, and not merely hearers who delude themselves.*
James 1:22

"Victory has a thousand fathers, but defeat is an orphan.
—John F. Kennedy (1917–1963)

*Rise up; this matter is in your hands. We will support you, so take **courage** and **do it**.*
Ezra 10:4

IN HIS CLASSIC BOOK, *THE RAISING OF A MODERN Day Knight*, Robert Lewis defined manhood as four progressing steps: "Rejecting passivity, accepting responsibility, leading courageously, and expecting a greater reward." This knowledge was monumental when I first read it. In a recent interview with Robert on the Men in the Arena Podcast he explained that each of the four components of manhood builds upon the previous. In other words, you cannot accept responsibility unless, or until, you reject passivity.

I agree wholeheartedly that **accepting responsibility** is critical to becoming a man. Any man who defers responsibility or displaces blame is less than a man and not the best version of himself that God requires.

Males retreat when the high call of fathering requires their full engagement. Males sleep in on Sundays while the family goes to church. Males refuse to do what is beneath their pay grade even if that means **remaining** unemployed. Males listen to the television more than their wives and children. Males refuse to embrace their God ordained responsibility to lead. Males pursue their hobbies more than their wives.

Men, however, respond to the responsibilities of the hour. They are responsible to lead. Look at the challenge to men in 1 Timothy 3:4-5: *"He must manage his own family well and see that his children obey him with proper respect. If anyone does not know how to manage his own family, how can he take care of God's church?"*

Look at Ezra's passion, *"Praying and confessing, weeping and throwing himself down before the house of*

God," because of the men who were, *"unfaithful to...God by marrying foreign women" (Ezra 10:1-2).*

Ezra took responsibility for the sins of those he was charged to lead!

It takes incredible courage for the leader to accept responsibility for the choices of those they lead. In the book *Extreme Ownership,* Jock Willink and Leif Babin write, "When subordinates aren't doing what they should, leaders that exercise Extreme Ownership cannot blame the subordinates.

They must look into the mirror themselves. The leader bears full responsibility. Put another way, when leaders experience a win, they should look out the window and give credit to their team. But when things go wrong, they should look at the mirror and critique themselves."

John F. Kennedy affirmed this leadership truth with, "Victory has a thousand fathers, but defeat is an orphan." Leadership takes undaunting courage and extreme ownership.

But accepting responsibility isn't enough without taking action *(Ezra 10:4).*

Response is the root of responsibility. Then in Ezra 10:4, Shecaniah the son of Jehiel exhorts Ezra to, "Rise up; this matter is in your hands. We will support you, so take **courage** and **do it**."

Did you catch that? Shecaniah was first recorded Nike commercial: "Just Do it!"

Who are you responsible to lead? Where do you need to respond to their struggles and help them win? Where have you sat by passively for too long while those you love suffer at their own hand? Where should you step up your leadership game? Where can you set aside your childish ways and take care of what and who has been placed **in your hand**?

Gut Check
Small Group Exercise

Reflect on Thomas Jefferson's statement that, "One man with courage is a majority."

How do you apply it to your family?

Discuss James 1:22 25 and how to apply it as a leader.

Where do you need to respond to their struggles and help them win?

How have you been too passive for too long?

What courageous leadership principles do you see in Ezra 10:1-17?

Part III - Courage, A Sign Of Strength

CHAPTER 21

VISIONEERING COURAGE

"He who wants to go fast travels alone.
He who wants to go far, travels together."
—N'gambai African Proverb

The Lord gave this command to Joshua son of Nun: "Be
strong and courageous*, for you will bring the Israelites*
*into the land I **promised** them on oath, and I myself will be*
with you."
Deuteronomy 31:23

"There are always difficulties arising that tempt you to
believe your critics are right. To map out a course of action
and follow it to an end requires some of the same **courage**
that a soldier needs. Peace has its victories, but it takes brave
men and women to win them."
—Ralph Waldo Emerson (1803–1882)

A<small>S A HIGH SCHOOL ATHLETE,</small> I <small>EARNED A VARSITY</small> letter to sew on my letterman's jacket. After subsequent varsity seasons I was awarded smaller, representative patches that were also sewn on the original letter. For example, a small football was awarded to represent one year of varsity football.

That's it.

Today's varsity athletes personalize their jackets by adding school mascots, favorite Bible verses, years of completion, and nicknames. Nick was a young man in my youth group who was a phenom with Major League Baseball. He knew all of the significant players, teams, and statistics like no other. Because of his great baseball knowledge, his peers gave him the nickname, "Editorial," which he boldly displayed on the back of his jacket.

When I get to heaven and talk to Joshua about his life verse, theme, or motto, I'm sure he will say, *"Be strong and courageous!"* Joshua began as Moses's aide *(Deuteronomy 1:37)* and finished as the leader of an entire nation. Can you imagine the courage he needed to follow Moses? Can you imagine the courage it takes to lead a nation? Think of all the criticism, ridicule, and maliciousness the leaders of nations are compelled to endure.

It takes great strength and courage to see past the minutiae of today to the big picture of tomorrow. Great dreams necessitate great fortitude. There is no glory without extreme guts. Courage is not the absence of fear, but the **presence** of the unseen.

In this section we address the third irrefutable attribute of courage—a sign of strength. Courage **is** a call to action. Courage **is** a choice. Later we will learn that for some, courage **is** a character trait. The third irrefutable attribute of courage **is** a sign of strength. Just as cowardice is an attribute of the weak, courage is associated with the strong.

No other man in Scripture is told to be strong and courageous more than Joshua and his generation. Notice also that whenever we see the phrase "be strong and courageous" it is a command to "be." It is a call to claim courage as a characteristic. A strong man, like a courageous man, has forged his strength through consistent acts of valor over time.

God constantly reminds Joshua to "be strong and courageous" throughout the book named after him in order to ensure his strength will endure through the many tests he would endure.

It is interesting to note that the last time we see these words, it's not God addressing Joshua, but Joshua encouraging the people. Joshua had made the transition from acting strong and courageous to **being** strong and courageous.

It became a part of his character.

Joshua saw the Promised Land conquered even back in Numbers 13 when every other spy except Caleb opposed him. He had a vision, and that vision took courage. It takes a courageous faith to see what others do not see. Hebrews 11:1 defines faith as, *"The assurance of things hoped for, the conviction of things not seen."* Sounds a lot like vision, doesn't it?

Faith takes the proverbial leap into the unknown even when fear tempts to paralyze. In the midst of fear, courage moves on faith. When fear tempts a man to hide, its faith that gives him the guts to put himself on display. Fear keeps us in the boat. Faith sees what no one else does and responds with the courage to walk on the water (Matthew 14:28).

Gut Check
Small Group Exercise

How do you see courage as a sign of strength?

Discuss the above Ralph Waldo Emerson quote.

What resonates the most with you?

Look at Proverbs 29:18 (King James Version) and Hebrews 11:1.

What similarities do you see between vision and faith?

How are they different?

Where have been obsessed with knowledge that took away from growing in biblical expertise?

Deuteronomy 31:23 speaks about the Promised Land.

What is your land of promise (Psalm 20:4)?

CHAPTER 22

LEADING COURAGE

"The whole earth is the tomb of heroic men and their story is not given only on stone over their clay but abides everywhere without visible symbol woven into the stuff of other men's lives."
—Pericles (495–429 BC)

Since we have gifts that differ according to the grace given to us, each of us is to exercise them accordingly...he who leads, with diligence.
Romans 12:6 and 8b

"Do not pray for easy lives. Pray to be stronger men.
Do not pray for tasks equal to your powers.
Pray for powers equal to your tasks."
—Phillips Brooks (1835–1893)

*Be strong and **courageous**, because you will **lead** these people to inherit the land I swore to their forefathers to give them.*
Joshua 1:6

Imagine it's the fourth quarter in the state championship football game of your senior year of high school. You've quarterbacked this team since your sophomore year, a three-year varsity starter. You're down by six points with two minutes left and one timeout. You've just received the punt and the ball rests on your twenty-three yard line.

You're ready for this moment. You've practiced the two-minute drill, special plays, and clock management a lifetime. You've dreamt of this moment since you were a sandlot quarterback. The fans are cheering, the scouts are watching, and your parents are praying. As you run onto the field, the coach grabs your shoulder and says, "You played a great game tonight son, but we're giving the little guy a chance to win this one."

He points to the freshman quarterback who was brought up for the playoffs to inflate the roster. He has never taken a live varsity snap. You sneer at him, but he doesn't see you. He is standing on the sidelines, helmet nowhere to be seen, laughing with his freshman buddies. He has no clue what's about to happen. He only knows the handful of varsity plays that he was limited to on the freshman squad.

After the shock wears off, he runs onto the field and calls the first play. The team, thinking their leader is injured, rallies around their inexperienced quarterback and marches **your** team seventy-seven yards in eight plays to win the game on a fade route to the corner of the end zone. An extra point later and your team wins the championship.

Does this sound too ridiculous to be true?

· · ·

This exaggeration reminds me of Moses's protégé, Joshua. We forget that Joshua was Moses's assistant (Deuteronomy 1:38), who Moses called off the sidelines to lead the Israelites into the Promised Land. Joshua could have fumbled. He could have shrunk back to cowardice. He could've deferred to Caleb.

But he didn't. He never flinched—not once—at the opportunity. No incident in Scripture **ever** reveals doubt in Joshua's mind or words. He just put on his helmet and got in the game. He didn't flinch because God never flinches. Listen to what God said to Joshua, "Be strong and courageous, because you **will** lead these people to inherit the land I swore to their forefathers to give them" (Joshua 1:6).

You **will** lead them. It's the same thing God tells every man. He points to your wife and children, then looks you in the eyes and says, "You **will** lead them."

God never doubts that you have what it takes. Neither should you.

Many once-brave men have been lost on the field of cowardice facing lesser challenges, by choosing to trust their strength and skills instead of God's timing and anointing. Courage is more than walking in obedience—it's running into the fray.

When God says it, that settles it.

But we aren't talking about eleven teammates, a couple thousand fans, and a high-pressure football game. With Joshua, we're talking about leading a nation of over a million people to an elusive "Promise Land" after forty years of failure and frustration. Can you imagine the pressure?

How does that pressure measure up to leading a wife, children, and grandchildren into the Promised Land of faith and commitment? God asked Joshua to be what amounted to the president of his nation. He's asking you to be the patriarch of your family. Comparatively speaking, you can do this! You **will** do this!

Gut Check
Small Group Exercise

Talk about people who have impacted your life because they answered God's call to, "Be strong and **courageous**, because you will **lead** these people."

What made them special to you?

Where is your father in this question?

Read God's words to parents in Deuteronomy 6:1-25.

What leadership principles do you see?

What did your parents teach you?

How will (or did) you parent differently?

What does this passage teach us about overcoming our fears to lead?

Deuteronomy 6:20-25 talks about the power of story and personal testimony in leading those we love closer to Jesus.

What stories do you have that might draw those you love closer to Jesus?

CHAPTER 23

TREMBLING COURAGE

"**Courage** is fire. Bullying is smoke."
—Benjamin Disraeli (1804–1881)

*Say to those with anxious heart, "Take **courage, fear not**.*
Behold, your God will come with vengeance;
The recompense of God will come, But He will save you."
Isaiah 35:4

"If we let things terrify us, life will not be worth living."
—Seneca (4 BC–65 AD)

*Have I not commanded you? Be strong and **courageous! Do***
***not tremble** or be dismayed, for the Lord your God is with*
you wherever you go.
Joshua 1:9

HAVE YOU EVER DONE THE RATTLESNAKE DANCE?
My Western Oregon friends are probably scratching their
heads in wonder. The climate of Western Oregon is not
conducive for rattlesnake survival. As far as I know, they
simply are not here. Not so, however, for outdoorsman
adventuring in the dry and rocky terrain of Eastern
Oregon, or of my hometown on California's Central
Coast.

I'm an avid outdoorsman who spends close to two
hundred days a year hiking, biking, and exploring
outdoors. Fear is close by whenever I'm in unknown
mountains. There's a lot that can go wrong and one must
be fully aware of all his surroundings: weather conditions,
predators, location, and terrain are among a few.

But whenever I'm in dry and rocky country,
rattlesnakes are near the top of my list. If you have even
done the rattlesnake dance, you know what I mean. The
mountains are a force to be reckoned with, but few things
make my adrenaline pump, legs jump straight up, and body
shake in terror like that brush thrashing, buzzing reptile.

Far more times than I care to remember, I've hiked
down a brush-covered game trail only to be rattled to the
core by the explosion of a nearby sage bush as a rattler
threatens to strike.

You've never seen something so hilarious as a grown
man jumping straight in the air (I get much higher than
you would think when a rattler is involved), screaming like
a giddy girl at a slumber party, only to hit the ground
dancing around the coiled viper, trying to avoid its strike.

. . .

It's the rattlesnake dance.

Even thinking about it sends chills up my spine.

One time I did "The Dance." I was on the Owyhee River in Eastern Oregon hiking back to camp faster than I should in rattlesnake country, when I almost stepped on the unsuspecting snake. I did my best Michael Jackson, jumping as the snake pulled back to strike. Then something strange happened.

As I hit the ground that pathetic snake, apparently even more terrified than me, buried its head in a nearby hole and refused to look at the giant figure dancing in front of it! I guess it figured if it didn't see me, I wouldn't see it!

Then I noticed its shaking tail was silent. It was a bullsnake! Common to the area, they look similar to a rattler but are not poisonous and obviously have no rattles. I literally dodged a bullet, or should I say bullsnake!

What many dancing hikers don't know is that rattlesnakes don't shake while hunting prey, only when they are afraid and feel threatened. Experts believe the rattle is a nervous warning to potential predators. The rattle is literally a reaction of "fear and trembling."

Maybe God gave the snake its rattles to teach men the power of God. The awesome power of a holy God should shake us up. It should, on a holy level, rattle us.

In Joshua 1:9 God commands Joshua; *"Have I not commanded you? Be strong and courageous! Do not **tremble** or be dismayed, for the Lord your God is with you wherever you go."*

Joshua was great because Yahweh was his greatest fear. He knew God was omnipresent in his life and circumstances, He trusted and feared God at the same time.

When a man's fear of God is greater than his greatest fear, then he is an unstoppable force. He is free to walk in radical obedience to the God he fears above all other things. We will never rise above the thing we fear the most.

The key is to fear something worthy enough, and Who is better to fear than the God of the universe? We are hindered when we step out **of** faith instead of stepping out **in** faith.

Whatever you fear more than God is an idol. Losing your job. Not being loved. The failure of a child. The terminal illness of a loved one. If you fear any of these more than stepping out into the "Land (God) will show you" (Genesis 12:1), it's an idol.

If you fear losing your wealth more than selling everything to follow Christ (Mark 10:21)? It's your god. If you fear leaving your career more than following the radical call of Jesus (Matthew 4:20)? It's your object of worship.

Whatever you tremble at more than you tremble at God **is** your god.

We view God too lightly. We fear God too little. We've deafened ourselves to the rattles and forgotten the venom. When we fear something more than God, we become like the men in Psalm 55:19, *"Who never change their ways."*

Action is often a guttural response to fear; "I'm walking on another trail, and I don't care how far out far of the way it is!"

We've grown soft because we tremble more at the things of the world than the things of God. The bravest of men trust God the most for we will only be as great as the object of our faith. One day every knee will rattle in fear before a mighty and awesome God (Philippians 2:10-12). I say the sooner the better. Let the fear of God shake you up now so you won't be rattled later.

Gut Check
Small Group Exercise

What do you think of the statement, "When a man's fear of God is greater than his greatest fear, then he is an unstoppable force"?

Look at Philippians 2:9-13. What do you see about fearing God?

How does cheap grace prevent us from fearing God?

Read the stories refenced in Genesis 12, Matthew 4:18-22, and Mark 10:17-31?

How would you respond in each of these three scenarios?

Discuss the statement that, "We are hindered when they step out **of** faith instead of stepping out **in** faith."

CHAPTER 24

COMMANDING COURAGE

"Give me one hundred preachers who fear nothing but sin, and desire nothing but God, and I care not a straw whether they be clergymen or laymen; such alone will shake the gates of hell and set up the kingdom of heaven on Earth."
—John Wesley (1703–1791)

*Then they answered Joshua, "Whatever you have **commanded** us we will do, and wherever you send us we will go. Just as we fully obeyed Moses, so we will obey you. Only may the Lord your God be with you as he was with Moses. Whoever rebels against your word and does not obey your words, whatever you may **command** them, will be put to death. Only be strong and **courageous!**"*
Joshua 1:16-18

On August 1, 1992 Shanna and I exchanged wedding vows in front of 300 friends and family members. The pastor convinced us to write our own vows, which I was in full favor of. Shanna, on the other hand, is not a fan of writing, let alone wedding vows. Our pastor's influence eventually won her over, along with his promise to help her.

I was excited to hear her heart. I was curious.

I exchanged my vows fist. They included most things that you would expect from a groom with one **massive** exception. Shanna refused to marry me unless I publicly vowed to pick up after myself around the house! True story. I gladly proclaimed my loving oath to the laughs of hundreds of people.

Knowing Shanna's insecurity about writing her own vows, my expectations were lower than they should have been, but she stole the hearts of all when she boldly vowed from book of Ruth, *"Where you go I will go, and where you stay I will stay. Your people will be my people and your God my God" (Ruth 1:16).*

She was 22. We were young and clueless. Who would have realized how deep her commitment ran? How could her young heart have known what God would asked her to do?

She never wavered.

While dating she told me, "I will live anywhere God calls us—except Los Osos or Morro Bay, California (my alma mater). I hate the fog. The streets are a nightmare since most of them are not through roads, and it's gray there all the time." Two years later God called us to a church in Los Osos where we served in the place fog was invented for nearly ten years. Our kids were dedicated in that church. Two of our sons were born there.

Some of our fondest memories happened during that season because Shanna fulfilled her vows. And I tried to keep the house clean in case you were wondering!

Ten years later, God called us to leave everything we knew and move a thousand miles to northern Oregon. She never flinched. She continued to ruthlessly trust the vision God had for our lives.

Nearly a decade later, she would be called upon again to follow me on an even greater adventure when we left the security of church employment to launch Men in the Arena from scratch, with no assistance, during one of the worst economies in American history.

All she said in response was, "I've trusted you for 20 years and you've never let me down, and I will keep trusting you."

She didn't follow because I commanded it. She didn't follow because I demanded it. She didn't follow at all. She trusted the voice of God in my life and abandoned her will to wholeheartedly partner with me on the journey. She is my hero.

It's one thing to trust God when he asks you to do something radical, but to trust your husband when God is calling him to what, statistically, had no way of succeeding without a miracle is courage beyond words. Her courage inspired me. God's faithfulness changed me.

Shanna is one of the bravest people I've ever known.

In Joshua 1:16-18, the Israelites are preparing to enter the Promised Land. The Reubenites, Gadites, and the half-tribe of Manasseh were preparing to fight with Joshua as promised. Afterward they would return to their inheritance **east** of the Jordan River.

I found their only request to Joshua intriguing:

*"Whatever you have **commanded** us we will do, and wherever you send us we will go. Just as we fully obeyed Moses, so we will obey you. Only may the Lord your God be with you as he was with Moses. Whoever rebels against your word and does not obey your words, whatever you may **command** them, will be put to death. Only be strong and **courageous!**"*

In other words, "Hey Josh, we're laying our lives on the line here. Don't blow it. Be brave and we'll follow. Be a coward and we'll die." I know, because this is what Shanna's vows said to me, and I feel the weight of those vows every day.

This is a critical element for men desiring to lead. A man can't lead others into the promises of God while paralyzed by fear. Your love for God and His mission **must** override your **fear**. And those following you must see it. Be unwavering in your faith that "Lord your God be with you."

Gut Check
Small Group Exercise

Discuss the words of John Wesley; "Give me one hundred preachers who fear nothing but sin, and desire nothing but God, and I care not a straw whether they be clergymen or laymen; such alone will shake the gates of hell and set up the kingdom of heaven on Earth."

Discuss the dialogue between Ruth and Naomi in Ruth 1:15-18.

What was at stake for Ruth?

What can you learn from Ruth's life?

Where else is she mentioned in Scripture?

What can you learn from her decision to follow Naomi?

Read 1 John 5:3. What commandments are more burdensome to you?

What mandates from Scripture do you struggle with the most?

Why?

CHAPTER 25

RESPONSIBLE COURAGE

"The majority is usually wrong."
—Chuck Swindoll (1934–present)

*Arise! For this matter is your **responsibility**, but we will be with you; be **courageous** and act.*
Ezra 10:4

"The Lord gets his best soldiers out of the highlands of affliction."
—Charles Spurgeon (1834–1892)

*(Hezekiah) appointed military officers over the people and assembled them before him in the square at the city gate and encouraged them with these words: "Be strong and **courageous**. Do not be afraid or discouraged because of the king of Assyria and the vast army with him, for there is a **greater power with us** than with him."*
—*2 Chronicles 32:6-7*

WHEN I WAS A YOUNG BOY, I WAS INVITED TO A neighborhood friend's birthday slumber party. We were shooting hoops the morning after our sleepover when Frank, the rowdiest neighborhood kid, thought it would be cool to climb through a high window of our elementary school that was habitually open. Frank, the smallest guy in the group, was the neighborhood bully, and the quickest kid in the neighborhood who had discovered that the big guys like me couldn't catch him no matter what he said.

He became an expert at beating up people with words. He used his oratory skills to convince each boy to join his felonious mission, but I would not budge. The group ruthlessly harassed me but eventually left me alone in the backyard as they headed to rob the school.

The birthday boy's dad saw me alone in the backyard and we shot awkward baskets while they were on their mischievous mission. Tight-lipped about their whereabouts, I silently shot baskets until I heard the phone ring inside.

It was the police.

The principal happened to be at school on that Saturday morning and caught all my buddies in the act. Busted! We all learned a valuable lesson that day. Mine was twofold: 1) do what is right even if the majority stands against you, and 2) the majority is usually wrong. Those two rules have served me well as a follower of Jesus Christ. I live by them to this day.

That story reminds me of a time I saw a Post-it note one of my youth group students had stuck on his mirror that said, "Me, plus God, is a majority."

. . .

Both remind me of King Hezekiah before battle in 2 Chronicles 32:6-7 when he encouraged his outnumbered troops to, *"Be strong and courageous. Do not be afraid or discouraged because of the king of Assyria and the vast army with him, for there is a greater power with us than with him."*

You, plus God, is a no-lose situation (Romans 8:28 and 37) no matter what the outcome is.

We need men like Hezekiah. We need to **be** men like Hezekiah, who modeled the kind of courage that comes from God. He had the courage that wasn't afraid to take a step of faith. It was the kind of courage that inspired courage in others (2 Chronicles 32:5) because the God-factor was always in play.

Christianity will always be a minority view. To stand for Jesus often means to stand alone. To stand firm with Christian values is to stand in the minority. To walk with Jesus is to walk through the narrow gate (Matthew 7:13-14). But it's the right gate. It's the only gate (John 14:6-7).

Just because you stand in the minority doesn't mean you should stop standing. It just means you should stand firm. If you don't have the guts to stand alone, then the long-term vitality of your faith is in jeopardy. If you don't have the confidence to trust the equation that you, plus God, is a majority, your belief is little more than cognitive assent. If you aren't willing to stand your ground against a majority world view, you are little more than a functional atheist who knows the right things about God but is unwilling to live according to the Word of God.

Gut Check
Small Group Exercise

What are your thoughts on John Wayne's comment, "True grit is making a decision and standing by it, doing what must be done. No moral man can have peace of mind if he leaves undone what he knows he should have done"?

Compare the people n Matthew 7:13-14 with those in Matthew 25:31-16.

What are some things you notice?

What do Romans 8:28 and 37-39 teach us about the power of God in the midst of adversity?

What did Hezekiah mean in 2 Chronicles 32:6 when he said, "for there is a greater power with us than with him"?

Where do you need to stand firm against the majority?

CHAPTER 26

MARCHING COURAGE

"It is easier to find men who will volunteer to die, than to find those who are willing to endure pain with patience."
—Julius Caesar (100–44 BC)

"So Joshua went up from Gilgal, he and all the people of war with him and all the valiant warriors."
Joshua 10:7

"When a brave man takes a stand, the spines of others often stiffen."
—Billy Graham (1918–2018)

ONE OF THE MOST EPIC BATTLES IN HISTORY IS chronicled in Joshua 10:1-28. Gibeon's fear of the Israelites and the deception of its leaders in order to secure an alliance with Joshua (Joshua 9:1-27) sets the stage. The five Amorite kings of the Hill Country formed an alliance of their own and moved in to attack Gibeon who promptly called out to Israel for help (vs 6).

A tactical genius, Joshua marched his most "valiant warriors" (vs 7) all night long and surprised (vs 9) the Amorites with a pre-dawn attack, throwing the groggy and ill prepared Amorites into confusion. In a panic they fled as the Israelites chased and slaughtered them.

As dawn approached, clouds filled the sky and boulder-sized hailstones rained down, striking only Amorite soldiers. More men were killed by hail that day than by Israelite soldiers (vs 11).

But the sky began to clear. The surviving Amorites must have breathed a sigh of relief as the sun rose in the east, but unknown to them their destruction was looming from the eastern sky.

Joshua looked up, lifted his arms, and prayed, *"O sun, stand still at Gibeon, and O moon in the valley of Aijalon" (vs 12).* What happened next has never been recorded since, *"So the sun stood still, and the moon stopped, until the nation avenged themselves of their enemies" (vs 13).*

The sun stood still until the slaughter of every Amorite was complete. All that remained were the five Amorite kings who by this time had hidden themselves in a cave. This is where it gets interesting. Joshua brings the kings out, throws them on the ground, and had his *"chiefs of the men of war" (vs 24)* place a foot on the neck of each king.

Imagine that your foot is pressed firmly onto the neck of a king. You're exhausted from an all-night march and all-day battle. You're coming off a massive adrenaline dump from a day of fighting. Your body is succumbing to extreme exhaustion. The blood of your enemies is sticky on your hands and face. Your forearms are locked up from wielding the sword that cut down dozens of men in battle. You can feel the heat of the sun baking the blood on your face as it stands still in the sky.

They say hindsight is twenty-twenty, which is why I believe Joshua saved his speech until now. His words seem misplaced. They are like a puzzle piece that doesn't fit—awkward, and confusing. Staring and the soon-to-be-executed kings Joshua says to his chiefs, *"Do not fear or be dismayed! Be strong and courageous, for thus the Lord will do to all your enemies with whom you fight" (vs 25).*

Why?

Why wait until now to say what he should have said before the battle?

Because Joshua was a great leader. Great leaders see beyond what others see. Joshua knew that the worst was yet to come. Southern Palestine had yet to be conquered (10:2-43), and Northern Palestine (11:1-29) would soon follow. Many battles would be fought, and many lives lost. Knowing this, Joshua wanted one thing seared into the hearts of his generals after the Battle of Five Kings: God will fight for you (vs 14).

The Promised Land conquest required the sign of strength that comes only for the man who trusts God implicitly. It's a question every man must answer, who is fighting for me? Like Joshua, Paul was convinced when he wrote, *"What then shall we say to these things? If God is for us, who is against us?" (Romans 8:31).*

Are you?

Does the world feel the heat of your burning conviction that God fights your battles? Do you possess that kind of courage?

Gut Check
Small Group Exercise

Share about a time you epitomized Billy Graham's quote, "When a brave man takes a stand, the spines of others often stiffen."

Read through the Battle of Five Kings in Joshua 10:1-28. What fresh insights do you see?

Why do you think Joshua waited until **after** the battle to tell his men to be "strong and courageous" (Joshua 10:25)?

What does Romans 8:31-39 mean to you?

Where are you overwhelmingly conquering right now?

CHAPTER 27

OBSERVANT COURAGE

"Cowards die many times before their actual deaths."
—Julius Caesar (100–44BC)

*You shall thus **observe** all My statutes and all my ordinances and do them; I am the Lord.*
Leviticus 19:37

"If you can't take it, you won't make it."
—Edwin Cole (1922–2002)

*May the Lord give you discretion and understanding when he puts you in command over Israel, so that you may keep the law of the Lord your God. Then you will have success if you are careful to **observe** the decrees and laws that the Lord gave Moses for Israel. Be strong and **courageous**. Do not be afraid or discouraged.*
1 Chronicles 22:12-13

PLAYING SCHOOLYARD SPORTS GROWING UP, WE often personified our favorite sports stars or superheroes. When playing schoolyard football, I imagined myself to be Hall of Fame linebackers Jack Lambert or Dick Butkus. On offense I was either Terry Bradshaw, Roger Staubach, or Larry Csonka, all of whom somehow made me bigger stronger, and faster than I really was.

If we were playing war in a nearby field my options were Audie Murphy, John Wayne, or Clint Eastwood —"You have to ask yourself one question. Do I feel lucky? Well, do ya, punk?" **I would like to stop here to say a special "Thank you" to those of you who served our country so I could play war as a child and not go to war like some of you did.** I stand for the "National Anthem" in your honor. You are the true heroes.

Whether it be Superman, Batman, or Spiderman, heroes are important to a young boy's childhood. They tell a story of valor in the face of adversity. We were blessed enough as children who grew up unhindered from the burdens of experience, pain, and trauma and were free to dream of becoming anyone or thing we wanted. And we always chose to be winners, heroes, and champions.

Why?

Because God designed men for greatness. He designed his sons to win. He designed men to change their world no matter how large or small because God knows that when a man gets it—everyone wins!

But greatness needs to be modeled. It needs to be observed in someone else. It needs a standard to follow. In the Word of God we not only see a recipe for greatness but for great courage. Men of conviction observe **and** obey God's Word and receive their modeling from God and His champions. Because of that, men who follow Jesus are some of the most courageous men in history— bar none.

In 1 Chronicles 22 we see an aging King David preparing for his death and the succession of his son Solomon to the throne. God told David that because of his warrior past, a history of great bloodshed, he would not be the one to build God's temple (vs 8). Instead, David's inexperienced son, Solomon, would finish the magnificent work.

But Solomon was young and unproven. David needed to call his greatness out because, "*My son Solomon is young and inexperienced" (1 Chronicles 22:5).* Solomon lacked proven courage, which we have learned is a personal choice, a character trait (over time), a call to action, and a sign of strength. Solomon needed all of the above to follow in his father's footsteps.

Traditionally, Israel was a nation of turmoil and war, but Solomon would be a man of peace and rest (vs 9). How could a peaceful man lead a historically warring nation? The answer was simple. God gave Solomon great *"discretion and understanding"* to lead the people of God into its greatest period of peace and prosperity. God planned to do great work through Solomon, but He had to first do a great work **in** Solomon.

Isn't that how it is when a man chooses to lead? God must do the work **in** him as He works **through** him. God changes the man who answers the high call to lead whether it is his family, church, or beyond. I promise you that the man changed the most by the Men in the Arena is the one banging on these keys! Leaders are readers. Leaders are learners.

Solomon observed and obeyed God's Word and became the wisest man to ever live, writing most of Proverbs and all of Ecclesiastes. Do you want to become a man of strength and courage? Good! Observe and do everything God commands. Dive into the deep end of God's Word. Study the lives of great men who have gone before you. Let Him do a great work **in** you so he can do a great work through you (1 Thessalonians 2:13).

Gut Check
Small Group Exercise

Which superheroes or sports stars did you idolize as a child and what truth does that speak to regarding manhood?

Why do children choose heroes not villains to imitate?

Give yourself a letter grade, A-F, based on Leviticus 19:37? Explain.

Look at Solomon's conversation with God in 2 Chronicles 1:7-13. Of all the thing she could have asked for—courage, wealth, and power, he asked for wisdom. How is wisdom better than courage?

How does wisdom lead to courage?

What is wisdom?

In Ecclesiastes 1:1-18 Solomon refers to seeking wisdom as, "Striving after the wind" (vs 14). How is wisdom greater than knowledge? What was Solomon's downfall in the end?

CHAPTER 28

WORKING COURAGE

In all labor there is profit, but mere talk leads only to poverty.
Proverbs 14:23

"I'm a greater believer in luck, and I find the harder I work the more I have of it...The three great essentials to achieve anything worthwhile are, first, hard work; second, stick-to-itiveness; third, common sense."
— Thomas A. Edison (1847–1931)

*David also said to Solomon his son, "Be strong and **courageous**, and do the **work**. Do not be afraid or discouraged, for the Lord God, my God, is with you. He will not fail you or forsake you until all the work for the service of the temple of the Lord is finished."*
1 Chronicles 28:20-21 NIV

EVERY GENERATION HAS ITS OWN TIMELESS sayings. I grew up as a teen in the '80s using phrases like, "Cool, stoked, gnarly, and totally awesome!" The other day I embarrassed myself with some 1980's vernacular when two young couples asked Shanna and me to take a picture of them that I verbalized, "Super cool!" Both couples repeated my comment laughing. I had aged myself.

More recently my youngest son, Colton, while convincing me to do something told me to, "Send it!"

"Huh?"

"You know dad. Send it. Go for it! Do it."

No. I didn't know. But now I do.

I remember another time when my oldest son caught me off guard with his Yoda-like (from Star Wars...I aged myself again) comment. After a hard day of training for football, my son James strutted into the living room, pounded his chest, and proclaimed, "I **did work** in the weight room today."

In my head I heard the Grand Master of the Jedi Order saying, "Work, I did. Hmmm."

James was talking about something many of us know —being in the weight room doesn't mean the work gets done. As a coach and a player, I was often mystified by athletes who showed up to the weight room to talk more than lift.

If you haven't gathered by now, courage takes **work.** The desire to be courageous is inherent in us but manifests only through personal choice during a threatening or precarious situation. Standing in the weight room will not make me strong but doing the work will.

· · ·

In an 1899 speech called *The Strenuous Life*, Theodore Roosevelt (1858–1919) said, "The work must be done; we cannot escape our responsibility; and if we are worth our salt, we shall be glad of the chance to do the work—glad of the chance to show ourselves equal to one of the great tasks set by modern civilization."

In 1 Chronicles 28:20 King David commissions his son Solomon to, *"Be strong and **courageous**, and do the **work**."* Solomon was a known a man of great wisdom. Wisdom is more than understanding. It is knowledge combined with the correct action. Google defines it as, "The quality of having experience, knowledge, and good judgment." Good judgment is synonymous with correct action.

Knowledge without action is slothfulness. Knowledge with incorrect action is foolishness. Of foolish behavior, John Wayne once said, "If you're gonna be dumb, you'd better be tough."

Strength doesn't result from comfort but strain, effort, and grit. The work must be done to keep courage up. Courage isn't sitting on the couch playing video games. It isn't the pastor hiding in the church office during the week while telling the church to evangelize their world on the weekend.

It isn't going with the flow. Its swimming upstream past those aimlessly drifting into redundancy. Dead things don't swim against the current. They drift.

Courage is a coarse piece of sandpaper rubbing against the grain. It presses on without excuse. It does work. Courage without action isn't courage at all—it's cowardice.

We all experience fear, but fear isn't cowardice until it fails to act. Cowardice justifies its immobility. Even the most frightened men become strong when they move forward in courage. Fear either **does nothing** or the wrong thing. Courage **does work**. Courage resists fear to overcome, which makes a man strong as well.

Courage shouts, *"How long will you lie there, you sluggard? When will you get up from your sleep? A little sleep, a little slumber, a little folding of the hands to rest"* *(Proverbs 6:9-10)*.

Choose courage by choosing to do the work.

Gut Check
Small Group Exercise

Summarize Proverbs 14:23 in your own words.

Compare Haggai 2:4 to 1 Chronicles 28:20. What relationship do you see between work and courage?

Part IV of this book is our final irrefutable attribute of courage—a sign of strength. What is the relationship between strength and work?

Where does your courage need work?

Where are you weak due to lack of effort?

Part IV - Courage, A Character Trait

CHAPTER 29

SIMPLICITY OF COURAGE

"It is **courage, courage, courage**, that raises the blood of life to crimson splendor. Live bravely and present a brave front to adversity."
—Horace (65–8 BC)

"Men fight for liberty and win it with hard knocks. Their children, brought up easy, let it slip away again, poor fools. And their grandchildren are once more slaves."
—D.H. Lawrence (1885–1930)

*Be strong and very **courageous**. Be careful to **obey** all the law my servant Moses gave you; do not turn from it to the right or to the left, that you may be **successful** wherever you go. Do not let this Book of the Law depart from your mouth; meditate on it day and night, so that you may be careful to do everything written in it.*
Joshua 1:7-8

How would you define success? Several years ago, I coached a high school football team that went 8-1. We were only one play away from a perfect season even though our Defensive Coordinator was on vacation. We lost that game 42-47 but were pleased with the results, considering that just two years before the team—under different leadership—finished a dismal 0-9.

Were we successful? It depends on how you define success. Success is subjective. It's difficult to define. For dozens of young men, parents, and the school, it was an overwhelming success. But the one young man who quit early in the season (and his angry parents) might think the season was a disastrous failure. The handful of athletes who never played football after that season might agree as well.

The demarcation of success depends on the perspective of the one defining it. Not only is it subjective but compartmentalized.

A successful businessman, for example may be highly efficient at making money but estranged from his children who view him as an absentee dad and workaholic. A celebrity may have millions of followers on social media and tons of money yet be suicidal. A professional athlete may have fame, money, and women, and be addicted to drugs or alcohol. A megachurch pastor may be on television, radio, and be famous while having an adulterous affair with his secretary. We see these scenarios play out in real time constantly. Success is subjective and compartmental.

Do you get my point?

Success is a matter of opinion.

. . .

Biblical success, however, is not compartmentalized. It permeates all areas of life, not one or two. It affects the whole man and everyone around him. When a man gets it —everyone wins.

John Maxwell's definition of success is closer, "Knowing your purpose in life, growing to your full potential, and sowing seeds that benefit others."

In Joshua 1:7, God commands Joshua to, "**be** strong and courageous," so he might find success wherever he goes. Later in this book we'll unpack courage's fourth irrefutable attribute—as a character trait, but it becomes a character trait only **after** courageous choices, compounded over time. A man of courage is the result of habitual, courageous choices over time.

This passage reveals a simple yet profound truth about courage. Do you want to be your most courageous version? Do you want to possess the elusive characteristic of courage that is only awarded to those brave souls who choose its path time after valorous time?

Why is it that many of the most courageous men in human history were devoted followers of Jesus? Why have so many of the greatest contributions to humanity come from believers in Jesus—Martin Luther, Galileo, Blaise Pascal, Nicolaus Copernicus, Johannes Kepler, Isaac Newton, Johann Sebastian Bach, Michelangelo, Rembrandt, J.R.R. Tolkien, C. S. Lewis, Frank Laubach, and Martin Luther King Jr., to name a few.

Do you want to be numbered among them?

Obey God's Word. God said it. That settles it. Simple. It is the easiest and most difficult thing you will ever do.

. . .

Courage only becomes a character trait when fear is removed as a temptation, and feelings become subservient to facts. Only when I am committed to Jesus at all costs (Luke 14:27), without personal opinions (John 12:24), or negotiation for personal rights (Galatians 2:20) am I free to live courageously even when under the mirage of fear.

Courage isn't the missing link of success. Obedience is! Any man who wears the veneer of courage without obedience to God's Word, is a shell of a man. He is like a warrior who cowers when called to fight for his marriage. He's like a jellybean, hard on the outside and soft and gooey on the inside.

It's easy to ignore God's Word when selfish feelings and personal rights are on the line. Radical obedience to God is difficult. Any man branded with the character trait of courage is a precious commodity. They operate above the rest. The characteristic of courage is for the whole man, the man of integrity, who has transcended his personal rights to wholly obey God.

Gut Check
Small Group Exercise

How do you interpret Joshua 1:7-8 in the context of Psalm 119:9-11 (above)?

Memorize Galatians 2:20. How would Paul explain its meaning to you?

What potential conflict can you distinguish between Galatians 2:20, Romans 7:14-25, and 12:1?

In Luke 14:25-35 Jesus admonished his followers to take up their cross to follow him.

Can you identify any areas where you have put the cross down and picked up your rights instead?

What is the context of John 12:24?

How do you apply it in your life?

CHAPTER 30

PROOF OF COURAGE

*We also exult in our tribulations, knowing that tribulation brings about perseverance; and perseverance, **proven** character; and **proven** character, hope; and hope does not disappoint, because the love of God has been poured out within our hearts through the Holy Spirit who was given to us.*
Romans 5:3-5

"We don't get to decide what happens to us, but we do get to decide how we will respond."
—J.R.R .Tolkien (1892–1973)

Then Azariah the priest entered after him (Uzziah) and with him eighty priests of the Lord, valiant men.
2 Chronicles 26:17

Being a man of courage—possessing the character trait of courage—is not inherent. It is neither implied or inherent throughout Scripture. It's earned one choice at a time, over time, for a lifetime. The possessor of courage is easily recognizable. He is a thermostat that others look to for guidance. He sets the bar. As Billy Graham once observed, "Courage is contagious. When a brave man takes a stand, the spines of others are often stiffened."

Our house has a thermostat and a thermometer. The thermometer **registers** the temperature by measuring the climate around it. The thermostat, however, **regulates** what that temperature will be.

The thermostat is the catalyst in controlling the climate. A man who has earned the title of "courageous" is similar. He is a regulator of climates. He is a change agent but let's be clear. You can act courageously momentarily but not be a man of courage. Remember the character quality of courage is earned over time, one courageous choice at a time. A courageous act regulates climate sometimes, but it is the constant fruit of a courageous man.

This is a slight but critical difference to note.

2 Chronicles 26 documents Uzziah's rise from a teenage king to a powerful ruler. The subtitle of 2 Chronicles 26:16-21 is, "Pride Is Uzziah's Undoing." Uzziah's undoing began in verse 17 when he entered the temple to break ceremonial law by burning incense. But Azariah followed him with eighty courageous priests of the Lord.

These eighty men weren't priests even though "priest" was the job title. There is a powerful principle here. Your job does not define you. God doesn't judge men by title, race, or status. He looks at the heart. Uzziah wrongly assumed that a bunch of non-threatening "Yes Men" followed him into the temple; instead it was a band of courageous God fearers, men who choice after choice, day after day, obeyed God's Word and in so doing became men of valor.

When Azariah stood against the sins of King Uzziah he didn't look for just any group of men. He looked for *m*en who possessed courage, a history of acting courageously in the face of fear. These men had a reputation of courage. They possessed the hard-earned character trait of valor.

These were climate-changers in God's house. Not Uzziah. Even though Uzziah possessed the title of King his hubris faltered in the presence of courageous men. If you're a spiritual leader of any kind—pastor, elder, deacon, other lay leader—there will be times when you will have to take a stand against the pride of a spiritual leader. There will be times you will have to confront a bully. Train yourself for that time by making courageous moves day in and day out so that when that day comes, you will naturally regulate out of a courageous character.

You either regulate or register. You are a thermostat or thermometer. Either is your choice. Do you want to be numbered among Azariah and his courageous men? Choose courage today and every day. Let courage weave through your character until it becomes an unbreakable rope of bravery.

Uzziah lived from that day on as a leper and ruled from a separate house (26:21) because brave men challenged his denigrating pride. Those nameless, courageous priests were catalysts of Uzziah's ~~to~~ repentance. He is eulogized in history as a man who, "did what was right in the eyes of the Lord" (2 Chronicles 27:2), and I have to wonder how much belongs to Azariah and the Courageous Eighty for his spiritual legacy.

Gut Check
Small Group Exercise

What is the difference between a courageous act and a courageous man?

Do you agree that the character trait of courage results from courageous choices compounded over time?

Explain.

How are they similar and easily confused?

Read 2 Chronicles 26:16-21. What other insights about courage do you see?

How are the men of Acts 6:3 like those of 2 Chronicles 26:17?

Read Romans 5:3-5. What are some ways you can prove your courage daily?

CHAPTER 31

STUBBORNNESS OF COURAGE

"The greatest accomplishment is not in never falling, but in rising again after you fall."
—Vince Lombardi (1913–1970)

"Do not be afraid to suffer. Do not be afraid to be overthrown. It is being cast down and not destroyed; it is being shaken to pieces, and the pieces torn to shreds, that men become men of might."
—Henry Ward Beecher (1813–1887)

*I will surely strike my hands together at the unjust gain you have made and at the blood you have shed in your midst. Will **your courage endure** or your hands be strong in the day I deal with you? I the Lord have spoken, and I will do it. Ezekiel 22:13-14*

MEN OFTEN CELEBRATE WITH SHAKING HANDS, high-fives, chest bumps, forearm pounds, knuckle punches (with explosion for effects of course), and the more recent Coronavirus elbow knock.

It's our way of affirming one another. We like to encourage one another with sayings like, "Send it! Keep it up. Bring the heat. You're crushing it." When God says, *"I will surely strike my hands together" (Ezekiel 22:13)*, you'd better wait for the **boom**. Ready or not, here it comes.

Courage is needed when God strikes His hands. It's the noise demanding our faith in a crisis. Some of the most courageous men I know are blue collar, hard-working men who are sold out for Jesus. They look like your average man, but don't let their "Average Joe" status fool you. These men are champions. They are the men in the arena. When a crisis comes, they are ready. They've been preparing for this moment for years.

Ezekiel, like many Bible heroes, was a man of courage. We know he possessed the character quality of courage from God's words in Ezekiel 22:14, *"Will **your courage endure** or your hands be strong in the day I deal with you? I the Lord have spoken, and I will do it."*

One attribute of courage is grit, which has been defined as the stubborn refusal to quit. The Bible's synonym for grit is *endurance*. Quitters lack courage because one attribute of courage is endurance. Look at Jesus's grit in Hebrews 12:1-3,

*"Therefore, since we have so great a cloud of witnesses surrounding us, let us lay aside every encumbrance and the sin which so easily entangles us, and let us run with **endurance** the race that is set before us, fixing our eyes*

on Jesus, the author and perfecter of faith, who for the joy set before Him **endured** *the cross, despising the shame and has sat down at the right hand of the throne of God. For consider Him who has* **endured** *such hostility by sinners against Himself, so that you will not grow weary and lose heart."*

In her book *Grit: The Power of Passion and Perseverance,* Angela Duckworth wrote, "At various points, in big ways and small, we get knocked down. If we stay down, grit loses. If we get up, grit prevails."

Based on the educational attainment by high achieving adults, grade point averages among Ivy League undergrads, dropout rate of West Point United States Military Academy cadets, and National Spelling Bee participants, Duckworth concluded that grit is a better predictor of success than raw talent and IQ.

In her research she observed that individuals identified as "high in grit" were able to maintain their determination and motivation over long periods despite experiences with failure and adversity.

Ernest H. Shackleton is another man who possessed unwavering courage. You can read about in the mind-blowing book about his Antarctic adventures appropriately titled, *Endurance.* Shackleton explored Antarctica four times, but the book chronicles the final 1914–1916 Trans-Antarctic Expedition adventure when their ship, The Endurance, was trapped in ice. Two years later they were miraculously rescued with no fatalities.

Shackleton's family motto was *Fortitudine Vincimus* —"by endurance we conquer."

· · ·

Courage isn't manufactured. It can only be called "yours" when you have proven your grit time after enduring time. Once that history is ingrained so deeply within, courage becomes part of your character. Like a cattle brand seared on the hide of bovine, the character trait of courage is branded after years of stubbornly refusing to throw in the towel amidst adverse conditions.

As shared earlier, proudly displayed on the bookshelf behind me is a "Most Courageous" trophy that testifies to a moment of time that I acted courageously. But the rest of my life will prove whether I am truly a courageous man.

Courage must be ingrained so deeply into the **character** that it becomes an identifiable trait—he is a man of integrity, loyalty, and courage—each of which are forged in the fires of testing over time.

National Football League great Alex Karras once said, "It takes more 'manhood' to **abide** by thought-out principles rather than blind reflex. Toughness is in the soul and spirit, not in muscles and an immature mind."

Strengthen the hands of courage by putting them to work in your daily routines. Form the habit of living courageously so when the hands strike, you'll be ready. When you die, you will be known as a man of courage.

Gut Check
Small Group Exercise

Discuss your reasons for why the Bible never uses *courage* to describe Jesus.

How does Hebrews 12:1-3 prove that Jesus was a man of unequivocal courage?

Read 2 Timothy 4:5. Why was this so important for Paul to pass on to Timothy?

What is the "perfect result" in James 1:2-4 (NASB)?

What does 2 Corinthians 4:8-10 teach about grit?

CHAPTER 32

DISCOVERY OF COURAGE

"Even when you are down, look up at what you must
defeat. Then get up and fight."
—Bruce Lee (1940–1973)

*You, my God, have revealed to your servant that you will
build a house for him. So your servant has **found courage** to
pray to you.*
1 Chronicles 17:25

"No man is more unhappy than he who never faces
adversity.
For he is not permitted to prove himself."
—Seneca (4 BC–65 AD)

*O Lord Almighty, God of Israel, you have revealed this to
your servant, saying, "I will build a house for you." So your
servant has **found courage** to offer you this prayer.*
2 Samuel 7:27

I WAS WARNED THAT IF I MISSED THE CAMP FROM the south, I'd head miles into the canyon and get lost for days. This happened several years before GPS units were popular and hunters relied on paper topographical maps, their compass, and landmarks to navigate. I left camp that morning fully intending to steer north when I came off the mountain. I usually hike into a hunting area in the black of morning, hunt all day, and return to camp after dark.

Northern California's Yolla Bolly Wilderness is vast and confusing in the pitch black of evening, especially when you've never been there before. I'd already missed the surveyor tape I set up ten hours earlier and was so concerned about staying on the northern side of the range that I overshot my mark and headed down the wrong ridge, missing my mark by being too far north. During the confusion, my headlamp died, and I fumbled in the moonless night to find two batteries.

I began to panic.

"Dang it! I'm lost!"

I sat down on a tree stump and worked through my STOP acrostic one letter at a time. Stop. Think. Observe. Plan. Although, if I'm honest my acrostic went more like this: sit, observe, think, **pray**. Either way, as soon as I relaxed, I remembered the radio in my pack for times like this.

I called into the darkness and heard laughter and a fire cracking on the other end of the radio, "Fire a shot so we know where you are."

Bang!

"Head straight down the ridge. You are close."

I'll never hear the end of this.

Fifteen minutes later a set of headlights greeted me along with an abusive amount of teasing. I learned that when lost, you must call out. Sometimes you must shoot out.

In 2 Samuel 7 we circle back around to David's prayer not because we are lost but because it has another principle to discuss.

> *O Lord Almighty, God of Israel*
> *you have revealed this to your servant*
> *saying, "I will build a house for you."*
> *So your servant has found courage*
> *to offer you this prayer.*

No one reading through David's life would ever doubt that he was a man of tremendous courage. He is one of the most courageous men in Scripture, killing a lion, bear, and giant with a sling before he was able to drive a chariot (1 Samuel 17:36). Flawed, yes, but David epitomized courage, nonetheless. In 2 Samuel 7 David teaches that sometimes even the bravest—those branded with the character trait of courage—in moments of weakness must rediscover it. Maybe a moral failure, the wound of a trusted friend, or the violation of someone once trusted forces courage underground for a season. Proven years of courage are not in question, but at some point, all experience the Valley of the Shadow of Death (Psalm 23) and must journey deep to awaken our sleeping courage.

. . .

Have you been in a place so dark you couldn't muster the courage to call out to God let alone your wife or friend? In the darkness of sin, sometimes we lose the desire to pray. Sin blinds our eyes to the Light of the World. The spirit struggles for joy. The heart is swallowed by shadows and forgets to pray.

I remember talking to man who had recently repented of adultery. This guy had a herd of children ranging from elementary to high school aged and openly spent several nights a week at the home of his mistress. His wife knew it. His children knew it. His church knew it. And he didn't care. His house was disastrous, and wife was near insanity because of it. The kids were dirty—their house looked like squatters lived in it. I was shocked the day I learned that she was married! And the man claimed to follow Jesus nonetheless!

Eventually this man experienced radical repentance that brought him back to Jesus, his wife, and children.

One Sunday he publicly shared that he was in such a dark place he didn't pray for over a year. Not one time. Hebrews 4:16 was a reminder, "*Therefore let us draw near with confidence to the throne of grace, so that we may receive mercy and find grace to help in time of need.*"

Darkness will do that.

The key to courage during the dark times when we feel lost is to turn (Acts 26:20). Rediscover your courage to turn to the God you betrayed. Turn from the darkness and face the God who's been forsaken but will never forsake you.

. . .

Reach through the darkness and find the light. Call out to Him. *"If we are faithless, He remains faithful, for He cannot deny Himself"* (2 Timothy 2:13).

Gut Check
Small Group Exercise

How can you relate to David's prayer in 2 Samuel 7:27?

Read Psalm 23:1-6. Share about a time you lost yourself in the darkness and how you found your way to the light.

Read and discuss Hebrews 4:15-16. Compare it to the Temptation of Jesus in Matthew 4:1-11.

Read Acts 26:19-21. What does true repentance look like?

Is there anything you need to turn from today?

How does 2 Timothy 2:13 encourage you today?

CHAPTER 33

RAGE IN COURAGE

"I set myself on fire and people come to watch me burn."
—John Wesley (1703–1791)

*On the other hand I am filled with power—With the Spirit
of the Lord—And with **justice and courage** To make
known to Jacob his rebellious act. Even to Israel his sin.
Micah 3:8*

"Whatever you do, you need **courage**. Whatever course
you decide upon, there is always someone to tell you that
you are wrong."
—Ralph Waldo Emerson (1803–1882)

*Absalom commanded his servants, saying, "See now, when
Amnon's heart is merry with wine, and when I say to you,
'Strike Amnon,' then put him to death. Do not fear; have not
I myself commanded you? Be **courageous and be valiant**."
2 Samuel 13:28*

GROWING UP I WAS BIGGER AND STRONGER THAN the other kids my age in the neighborhood. My parents taught us that fighting was not okay, unless if there are no other viable options available. I grew up close to my younger brother and sister who, although we were only a couple of years apart, were both much smaller than me.

I distinctly remember the day Dad pulled me aside and said, "Son, I know I told you to avoid fights at all costs, but there is one exception. If anyone ever threatens your brother or sister, you have my permission to beat them up."

I was barely four years old.

A short time later a local bully named Ricky brought my little brother to tears. But Ricky made the mistake of allowing me to witness it. Seeing my rage, he sprinted for the safety of his home and his deputy sheriff father. I remember chasing him all the way to his yard, catching him just as he reached his front porch, and punching him so hard in the face that I bloodied his nose and lip.

After Dad congratulated me for defending my little brother, he made me apologize to Ricky whose bloody face was being treated by his giant law enforcement father. He is one of only two people I have ever hit. Both received bloody noses as a payment for picking on my little brother.

I'll never forget Dad's words, which carried into my adult life where violence is frowned upon, but justice is demanded to protect the world from the cowards we call bullies.

Something fierce wells up when I see a bully—dare I call it rage? A study of the root of the word courage shows that its root is *cor*—the Latin word for heart. In one of its earliest forms, *courage* meant "to speak one's mind by telling all one's heart."

Courage is a heart word.

But you can't spell courage without "rage." As we have seen through this book, two of the four irrefutable attributes of courage are: 1) it's a choice, and 2) it's a call to action. Both potentially involve highly emotive situations. I was not being nice, calm, or polite when I punched Ricky in the face. I was a raging bull. I was pissed that an older bully picked on my little brother.

There is a rage that must be controlled (Galatians 5:22-23) when the bully raises his cowardly head. When identifying this as a part of God's character and nature, this is called wrath. To teach this very real biblical characteristic of God, that many do not want to hear about, I created an acrostic for **wrath**—wreaking righteous anger towards humanity.

Wrath is God's righteous anger. Its goal is always kingdom centric and under control. It was righteous anger that compelled Jesus to make a whip and drive the vendors out of the temple court in John 2:13-25. "Indignant" at the suffering and exclusion of the man with leprosy, Jesus healed him (Mark 1:41). Again, in Mark 10:14 we see an "indignant," very angry, Jesus because the disciples were not letting the little children run to him. I argued with one pastor who vehemently believed anger is a sin and Jesus would **never** get angry. I asked hm about John 2 where Jesus drove out the money changers with a whip and quoted Ephesians 4:26, *"In your anger do not sin: Do not let the sun go down while you are still angry."*

He had no answer.

Anger is the dark side of following Jesus. It's the side of Jesus that nice Christians don't like to talk about. It seems so unholy. But talk to anyone who is passionate about for a Godly cause and you'll find anger lurking behind injustice. Wrath (wreaking righteous anger towards humanity) is the backhand of God's love just as Grace (God's riches at Christ's expense) is the softer side that reaches out to humanity. Both have the same end in mind but with obviously opposite expressions. If this life doesn't create a deep-seated wrath towards the evils of this world, then you need to check your heart.

Better yet, check your pulse.

Are you alive? Are you alive in Christ?

If so, God has planted a passion for something deep within that manifests as anger when you witness it—a child being harmed, the unborn being murdered, the mistreatment of others based on color, demographics, or politics?

Name your poison.

I love what Jesus said in Matthew 11:12, *"From the days of John the Baptist until now the kingdom of heaven suffers violence, and violent men take it by force."* I interpret this as the darkness doesn't push itself back. It doesn't wave a white flag and await further instructions. For this world to be impacted by the light, darkness must be violently dispelled through prayer and force.

Men in the Arena was launched when I saw the great injustices projected upon real men for the actions of worthless males masquerading as men. I saw men vilified by the media. I saw them marginalized by the Church. And I saw men minimized by a society that calls them toxic. In a coffee shop in Sisters, Oregon, I chose to give my life to help males become their best version of a man. Under the courageous call we answered, if I am honest, is outrage.

We are outraged by the vilification and marginalization of men. We are undone by the pain males have inflicted on this world, ignorant generalization of distorted masculinity projected upon good men, and strategic budget minimization by church leaders. Every day since has been a violent push against darkness fueled by a heart for men and an outrage at the systematic marginalization of them.

From the years 1960–1963, two-hundred and twenty episodes were produced of the popular cartoon, *Popeye the Sailor*. Popeye was a weak and crusty little sailor with huge forearms, a corn pipe, anchor tattoos, and a right eye that never opened. He loved his girlfriend Olive Oyl and had the ability to take a lot of abuse from his nemesis, Bluto. I anticipated every cartoon, knowing that at some point, Popeye would reach the point where he was done taking abuse, "That's all I can stand. I can't stand it no more!"

A can of spinach would mysteriously appear from his form fitting shirt and transform his weak body into a frightening exhibition of strength and aggression. You would think that after 200 episodes Bluto would learn, but he never did.

In 2 Samuel 13 we read about the rape of Tamar (vs 14) by her brother Amnon and Absalom's retribution two years later when he had Amnon murdered (vs 28). Though I am opposed to vengeance (Romans 12:19) and will not recommend righteous violence unless there is no other option, 2 Samuel 13 teaches us about courage and justice.

· · ·

John Eldredge believes that every man has a "battle to fight" and I couldn't agree more. But full-grown males aren't men yet. They have no cause to care about or injustice to declare war against it. They are neither hot nor cold. They are tepid, timid shells of masculinity. Their end is themselves and their goal is personal satisfaction, pleasure, and comfort (Philippians 3:18-20).

I pray that something ruins you. I pray that God wrecks you over something greater that yourself. I pray that God gives you a Kingdom assignment that outrages you, possesses you, and consumes you. I pray you have a Popeye Moment. The sooner the better.

Gut Check
Small Group Exercise

Where do you give your money, prayers, and time?

What hill will you die on?

What is your Popeye Moment?

Share about how you are currently fighting for your cause.

How do you explain God's wrath and God's grace?

How are they similar?

Different?

Read about Amnon, Tamar and Absalom in 2 Samuel 13. What did Absalom do right? What did he do wrong?

How would you have handled the situation?

How do you interpret Matthew 11:12?

CHAPTER 34

GOODNESS OF COURAGE

"You have enemies? Good. That means you've stood up for something, sometime in your life."
—Winston Churchill (1874–1965)

Be on your guard; stand firm in the faith; **be men of courage***; be strong. Do everything in love.*
1 Corinthians 16:13-14

"Until the day of his death no man can be sure of his **courage**."
—Jean Anouilh (1910–1987)

THE FIRST TIME I HEARD A MAN ADDRESS ADULT males as boys was at Family Life's "Weekend to Remember" couple's retreat. The speaker slapped my idea of manhood in the face. It was the first time I realized that I sometimes act like a boy instead of a man. There I realized many of the disputes I have with my wife revolve around childish behaviors like selfishness, impatience, and laziness.

I was forty years old at the time.

I'm tempted to be selfish, fail to accept responsibility, and choose pleasure over sacrifice. I know a lot of other forty-year-olds who often act like boys. I know eighty-year-olds who fit this description. I'm sure you do too.

As shared earlier, age doesn't make the man. Anatomy doesn't equate to manhood. Wealth, fame, and status don't either. Actions do.

When tempted to revert to childish behavior, we negotiate whether we will play the man or act the boy. Men, however, catch themselves in a vulnerable moment, repent and adjust. Boyish behavior is self-serving, egocentric, and immature. Boys are parents but **not** fathers, spouses but **not** husbands, acquaintances but **not** friends. They are Christians but are **not** disciples.

When we launched our ministry, Men in the Arena, our critics lamented that we weren't evangelistic enough. The truth, however, is that most males in churches are anonymous consumers who lack the maturity and responsibility to be listed among the men of the church. Their only value added is another number counted for Sunday attendance reports. They are liabilities not assets. Sunday morning males must be the target of our preaching, programs, and preparation. Sunday mornings are packed with low hanging masculine fruit for those willing to take it. When a man gets it—churches win.

Failure to strategically target men is the big miss in the church.

In my vocational ministry experience dating back to 1990, over three quarters of the men I served with as pastors are no longer in vocational ministry. Not even one of my senior pastors retired in full-time ministry. A handful disqualified themselves. Others simply burned out, walked away, or found a job with less of a headache and better compensation.

To answer the question whether our ministry is evangelistic, yes! And our mission field is men in churches who may call themselves Christians but aren't actively pursuing Jesus. Being a man takes courage. God calls men to be courageous leaders in the home, guarding against the enemies' attacks.

Knowing this, we must be careful not to use our Christianese, telling men they must accept Christ to be a real man. This is simply not true. I know horrible dudes who claim to follow Jesus. Conversely, I know great men who do not believe in God at all. Similarly, believing a man must follow Jesus to be a man of **courage** is not only ridiculous but historically and ethically false. How many times have we seen courageous "Christian" men decimate innocent lives and violate those who love them because of hubris and hedonistic choices? On the other hand, how many seemingly irreligious men live day in and day out sacrificially for those they love? Courage does not discriminate based on faith but makes choices that benefit others.

Most would agree that much of the world's pain and suffering are caused by the male gender. Males are the problem. Men are the solution. Where are the magnum men in the Church? Where is their leadership? Those guys are modern day heroes. We salute you if you are that man. This book is dedicated to you!

In 2 Corinthians 5:6-9 we see another reference to courage as a character trait, "Therefore **being always** of good courage..." It is one of only two times in Scripture we see good associated with courage, and both are in this passage:

*"Therefore, being always of **good** courage, and knowing that while we are at home in the body we are absent from the Lord— for we walk by faith, not by sight—we are of **good** courage, I say, and prefer rather to be absent from the body and to be at home with the Lord. Therefore we also have as our ambition, whether at home or absent, to be pleasing to Him."*

Our history books are filled with stories about men accomplishing courageous acts such as exploring new lands, crossing oceans, climbing mountains, and fighting for nations. But bravery and manhood are not mutually inclusive. In fact, many of these brave acts just mentioned ruined the lives of many through murder, neglect, divorce, abuse, or all the above.

What is my point of all this? Here it is. Courage takes on two forms—good and bad. This important to note— not all courage is good.

In 2 Corinthians 5:9 we see the difference between good and bad courage: *"Therefore we also have as our ambition, whether at home or absent, to be pleasing to Him."*

Men of "good courage" are driven by their desire to please God. Men of bad, or evil, courage are driven by ego, selfishness, and narcissism. Men come in many shapes, sizes, colors, political views, and demographics. I know myriad men who may not look "manly" outwardly but are some of the bravest, most selfless men I know. I am proud to call them friends.

I know of other brave men who are "manly" looking, strong and could rip my face off with their teeth, but their bravado is like a weapon of mass destruction for those who love them. Of them we get the phrase "toxic masculinity."

The man of **good** courage has God at the center of all his ambitions. His deepest desire is to put Jesus on display in everything. *"But may it never be that I would boast, except in the cross of our Lord Jesus Christ, through which the world has been crucified to me, and I to the world" (Galatians 6:14).*

His mettle is proven by pleasing God: *"Do nothing from selfishness or empty conceit, but with humility of mind regard one another as more important than yourselves; do not merely look out for your own personal interests, but also for the interests of others" (Philippians 2:3-4).* What kind of courage are you producing? Good? Bad?

Gut Check
Small Group Exercise

What are your thoughts that courage can be either bad or good depending on the fruit it bears?

What are some differences you see between good and bad courage?

How have you seen bad courage ruin lives?

Read 1 Corinthians 16:13-14. Where do you see good courage?

Which of the five items listed is a growth area for you?

What is your take-away from 2 Corinthians 5:6-9?

Philippians 2:3-4 doesn't mention courage but where do you see courage in it?

What selfless thing can you do this week?

How does Galatians 6:13-14 encourage you to press into the fruit of good courage?

CHAPTER 35

WILLS OF COURAGE

"Cowards die many times before their deaths; the valiant never taste of death but once."
—William Shakespeare (1564–1616)

"Lives of great men all remind us, we can make our lives sublime, and, departing, leave behind us, footprints on the sands of time."
—Henry W. Longfellow (1807–1882)

*The Lord gave this command to Joshua son of Nun: "Be strong and **courageous**, for you will bring the Israelites into the land I promised them on oath, and I myself will be with you."*
Deuteronomy 31:23 NIV

In this short passage Moses celebrates his one hundred and twentieth birthday. With God's help, Moses grew to become one of the most courageous men in history (Exodus 3:1-22). On his final birthday he delivers a speech on courage, directly referencing seven **"wills"** of valor. Each of these seven lessons about courage were learned on Moses's journey from being a Midian desert shepherd to becoming the deliverer of the Hebrew nation numbering well over a million souls.

"The Lord your God himself will cross over ahead of you" (vs 3). What a great lesson to learn about courage! There's no place God will send you that He hasn't been. From the mountaintop (Matthew 4:8 and 17:1) to the valley floor, God is with us (Psalm 23:1-6). It is impossible to escape from His presence (Psalm 139:7).

God is omnipresent. Because God is not limited by time, to Him the past, present, and future are indistinguishable. He can be anywhere at any time, at all times. He is present in painful memories, present circumstances, and future goals. There is nowhere that God is not.

"He will destroy these nations before you" (vs 3). There is no obstacle God can't move. There is no problem so big He can't solve. There is nothing remotely comparable to God. The bigger question is, will we trust Him even when He allows the obstacles to remain? Will we trust Him even if the obstacle continues to burden us?

I love the perspective of Meshach, Shadrach, and Abednego as the fiery furnace was being prepared to roast them, *"If it be so, our God whom we serve is able to deliver us from the furnace of blazing fire; and He will deliver us out of* *your hand, O king. But **even if He does not**, let it be known to you, O king, that we are not going to serve your gods or worship the golden image that you have set up" (Daniel 3:17-18).*

Contextually speaking, this was true for the Hebrews under Joshua's leadership, but it isn't always the case. Sometimes the boulders don't move. Sometimes the walls stay up. God is not some cosmic Bulldozer Dad who knocks down every obstacle in our path. But He will destroy the strongholds in our life so we can walk in freedom, love, and courage. We can trust *Romans 8:28* that, *"In all things God works for the good of those who love Him, who have been called according to His purpose."* He is faithful to lead us not into destruction but *"deliver us from evil" (Matthew 6:13).*

God has the power to transform even the most broken moments into a beautiful mosaic. Joseph was dealt a bad hand. He was abused by his brothers, hauled off to a foreign land, thrown into prison—and forgotten. But God used his pain to change the world. Later in life he held power of life or death over the brothers who abused him, but chose God's way instead; *"As for **you** (my emphasis), you meant evil against me, but God meant it for good in order to bring about this present result, to preserve many people alive" (Genesis 50:20).*

"You will take possession of their land" (vs 3). We must look at these promises through spiritual eyes since they refer to a specific time in history. These were literal promises for Joshua and the people, but it is not always the case. Courageous men must see what others fail to see.

Courageous men see the big picture. They see the invisible land they will possess (Colossians 1:6).

In 2 Kings 6 the Arameans surround the city in an attempt to capture Elisha. His attendant was terrified by what he saw, but Elisha saw beyond physical reality praying, *"'O Lord, I pray, open his eyes that he may see.' And the Lord opened the servant's eyes and he saw; and behold, the mountain was full of horses and chariots of fire all around Elisha. When they came down to him, Elisha prayed to the Lord and said, 'Strike this people with blindness, I pray.' So He struck them with blindness according to the word of Elisha. Then Elisha said to them, 'This is not the way, nor is this the city; follow me and I will bring you to the man whom you seek.' And he brought them to Samaria" (vs 17-18).*

Our plans are not God's plans and our ways are not His ways. Tertullian (155–220 A.D.), a second century Christian author from Carthage, Africa, understood this when he said, *"Plures efficimur, quitiens metimur a vobis: semen est sanguis Christianorum."*

"The blood of the martyrs is the seed of the church."

Like Elisha, Paul prayed that the eyes of our hearts would be opened (Ephesians 1:18) to see the world as it **really** is, a shadow of the reality to come. He later taught that the things we see are only temporal but that which we do not see is eternal (2 Corinthians 4:18). We must fix our eyes on what is unseen in order to see the universal picture.

Jesus looked dead on the cross. His death appeared to be catastrophic failure to the young men who left their careers to follow him. Friday was devastating but Sunday was coming!

"Joshua also will cross over ahead of you, as the Lord said" (vs 3). Moses was a great leader. What would the people do now? How would they replace him? But God had been preparing Joshua as the next leader since his youth. God transformed Joshua from aide, to general, to leader of the Hebrew nation.

God equips those He calls. It is amazing to watch God equip those who partner with His mission. We see it over and over again.

"And the Lord will do to them...whom he destroyed along with their land" (vs 4). God will do what God will do. The courageous man understands that God is God and he is a mere man (Ecclesiastes 5:2)—a spec in eternity. God's ways are higher than our ways and His thoughts are higher than our thoughts (Isaiah 55:9). Though we may not understand God's ways, He still demands our obedience.

If God chooses to deliver us to victory, we will praise Him. And if He does not, we will still praise Him. We praise Him for Who He is. We thank Him for what He does.

"The Lord will deliver them to you" (vs 5). Deliverance comes in many forms and it up to the courageous man of God to discern what that is. In Matthew 4:1-11 Jesus is led into the wilderness "by the Spirit" (vs 1) to be tempted by the devil where he was without food for forty days.

Two chapters later in Matthew 6:1 He teaches the disciples to pray, *"And do not lead us into temptation, but deliver us from evil."* In a couple chapters we see the Spirit leading Jesus into the wilderness to be tempted by the devil. Which is it? Did the Spirit **tempt** or **test** Jesus? Does God ever tempt someone to do evil (James 1:13) or does God refine us through constant testing?

Yes, the Bible says that the godly in Christ will be persecuted (2 Timothy 3:12). Yes, God commands that we do not vindicate ourselves but allow vengeance to be the Lord's *(Romans 12:9).* And yes, in 1 Corinthians 10:13 God promises that he will provide an opportunity for deliverance every time we are tempted, which brings me to my point. Here is a clearer perspective. How many times have you needed deliverance from yourself more than from an outside tempter? A thousand to one? A million to one? More?

Did the devil **really** make you do it? Or, was it your own evil desires that led you astray?

Your biggest enemy is the man you shave with every day. Ask God to deliver you from that guy!

"The Lord your God goes with you; he will never leave you nor forsake you" (vs 6). Lastly, when all else fails in life, God is love, God is good, and God is our Father. God will never set you up to fail for failure's sake. God is never to blame. In this life we will all experience pain, death, and loss. These things are immanent.

Pain is never an end in itself, but a way to grow. Even the courageous feel abandoned at some point. We have the presence of a loving God who, *"Comforts us in all our affliction so that we will be able to comfort those who are in any affliction with the comfort with which we ourselves are comforted by God" (2 Corinthians 1:4).*

The true tragedy in life belongs to those who suffer this life alone, without Jesus and without hope. With the sins of the world heaped on his shoulders (1 Peter 2:24) Jesus became a reproach to God (Isaiah 59:2), who abandoned him on the cross. That reproach was a pain greater than any physical pain he could endure, crying out, *"My God, My God, why have You forsaken Me?" (Mark 15:34).*

Because of the cross, God has promised to never leave one of His children.

Whether you experience the thrill of victory or the agony of defeat, God will never leave you hanging. In fact, *"He will never leave you nor forsake you" (Hebrews 13:5).*

Gut Check
Small Group Exercise

Review the seven "Wills" of Deuteronomy 31:1-6. Which one stands out the most to you and why?

Read Mathew 4:1, 6:13, and James 1:13. How do you mesh the three and remain theologically sound?

Read 1 Corinthians 10:13. What is your greatest temptation right now?

What secrets are you keeping that if they were discovered might ruin you?

How can you be delivered from your greatest temptation?

What tools do you have in place?

La Isla Bonita

On June 3, 2012, I stepped away from my pastoral position after more than two decades of full-time youth ministry to launch what is now Men in the Arena. We had no seed money, no lead pastor experience, and no megachurch fame. All we had was a dream and 15 men meeting weekly in a coffee shop.

I knew it was what God wanted, but to be honest, I saw no way we would ever change a nation, let alone raise the sixty-thousand dollars a year to make our first annual budget. I knew God wanted us to launch this ministry, but I neglected to share with Shanna that I thought God wanted to test my faith by asking me to do something He knew would fail. Would I trust Him in failure? Did I love Him enough to drop my nets and follow regardless?

The answer was a hesitant, "Yes?"

What did we do? We took the last vacation before the immanent foreclosure of our house, declaring bankruptcy, and leaving town with our proverbial tails between our legs. In celebration of our pending financial demise and my son's high school graduation (we did family trips for each graduation) we flew to the tropical paradise of San Pedro, Belize, on the Caribbean Island Ambergris Caye. Legend on the island has it that San Pedro is the subject of pop star Madonna's 1986 hit, *La Isla Bonita*. We planned to vacation with some family friends, then meet up with the church I just resigned from, for a weeklong youth mission trip.

To add insult to injury, I injured my back a few weeks before, which would require back surgery nine months later. To make matters worse, I lacerated my index finger on the gill plate of an Angelfish (long story), and because of high blood pressure couldn't stop the bleeding. The next two weeks in paradise were spent nursing a pulsating index finger, battling vicious mosquitoes, limping along with sciatica, and being terrorized by the thought of our return to the mainland when I'd be forced to face the reality that I had thrown my innocent family onto a sinking ship!

I was walking in fear like never before. My faith was wavering. My body was broken. I needed to find every ounce of courage I could, then muster up some more. This book, in its journal form, saved my life.

No. It changed my life.

Let's review what we learned so far about courage.

Courage is a call to action. In November 2010 while drinking coffee and reflecting on life in Sisters Coffee Company (Sisters, Oregon), God called me to men's ministry. Looking down at my cup, a quote caught my eye. I have been collecting quotes for all of my adult life, but this one caught my eye. It was written by the second century monk, St. Irenaeus (130–202 AD), who said, "The glory of God is man **fully** alive."

My life verse of John 10:10 had become obscured after years of being married, raising our family and the pressures of full-time ministry. John 10:10b had faded into the fog of dreams gone by. *"I have come that they may have life, and have it to the full" (NIV).*

After reading that coffee cup quote, I heard the unmistakable whisper of God: "I have just changed your heart."

I knew this call from God would ruin my safe and secure, though mundane, existence. Isn't that the problem with the mundane? It is packaged in a safe and secure portfolio. I tested the waters in January 2011, when I recruited 15 buddies from 19-70 years old and started a Bible Study at 6:00 a.m. every Tuesday in a local coffee shop. It was my initiation into men's ministry. It was the conception of what is now Men in the Arena. It was my putting the call into action.

Courage is a personal choice. A life-changing moment was pending. I knew it. I was in a dilemma, working full-time as the Associate Pastor over Youth Ministries at a small-town church, but I was no longer called to youth ministry. Every day felt like I was robbing the church. I found myself bound by a career I was no longer called to. My church deserved better than my rote ministry efforts. My calling had changed. My passion had changed. My life was about to be turned upside down.

Momentum increased as the "Original 15" men in my small group got more excited about what was happening in their lives. Their wives were ecstatic at the changes they were seeing. I really was called to minister to men, the evidence said. Would I move laterally in the church and take on this new role? The Church Board almost laughed at the thought during such a poor economy. Next I pitched the idea of becoming the heir apparent for a tired pastor. I was already preaching once a month because of a Board mandate. This sounded like the most logical next step, but I was told afterward that I, "Had a lot of (guts) to say that. You will be turning in your resignation next week." But the Board refused to call it a resignation and refused to pay unemployment, claiming I resigned based on my forthrightness that God had changed my calling.

That didn't go over as planned! But God knew.

At the news of my "dismissal" the District Superintendent was like a Grizzly bear over a fresh kill, licking his chops and begging me to plant a church. He even spent a lot of money for Shanna and me to fly to a church planters training and assessment in New Mexico. But planting a church or taking a church were too clean cut. In my heart I knew what I supposed to do—the hard thing. The impossible thing.

I chose the trail less traveled, the impossible path, to launch a ministry from scratch. I chose to override my terror and trust God for whatever he had in store, which I feared would be, "No Bueno." Not good.

It was the most courageous choice of my life. Or the dumbest one!

Courage is a character trait. Every spiritual gift test I had ever taken listed "Leadership" at the top of my profile, but the call to youth ministry compelled me to a second-chair role. I had never led, let alone started an organization before. My sons started calling me their "entrepreneur dad" but I felt more like their idiot dad. There's a fine line between courage and stupidity.

Something interesting happened after I announced my resignation. Money started showing up in our P.O. Box. Not enough to pay the bills of course, but more than my small faith expected. People started saying things like, "I've never seen someone go all in like this before."

One couple stood up at our send-off party saying, "We have never experienced someone launching a new ministry. We want to be a part of it!" They began supporting us with a large gift every month."

Overnight Shanna and I were elevated to a sort of celebrity status. Everyone wanted to watch this courageous new power couple to see if we'd sink or swim. Some of it was quite morbid. It was like flies gathering around a flame. It was like people slowing down on the highway to view an accident and we were in the wrecked car! All eyes were on us. I was instantly respected by senior pastors who months before saw me as a second-rate associate minister. Now they were inviting me to preach in their churches. Men wanted to meet for counseling. Others wanted to partner with our vision. The world opened up. I became a man of courage overnight.

It was becoming clear in my own experience that when a person acts courageously, compounded over time, they are transformed into a person of courage—it becomes a character trait.

Courage is a sign of strength. As shared earlier, it only took three months for the bank to come after our house. Two missed payments and the multi-colored foreclosure notices and the aggressive phone calls started coming. God ultimately redeemed our home at a lower rate!

A miraculous thirty-thousand-dollar gift was given from an unsuspected, unsolicited source and the year ended with the Board blessing us with the most substantial Christmas bonus of my ministry career. Also unsolicited. I bought Shanna her first bedroom set after more than 20 years of marriage. We had used my great grandmother's previously. Those two events solidified my faith in God, made me realize this ministry wasn't going away like I originally thought, and empowered me with an obvious new strength and fervor.

Four years later on October 3, 2016 my mettle would be tested again. While I was driving to a mule deer hunt in Eastern Oregon, my Board Chair called to inform me that our account was down to $489.29 with payday a week away. By this time, there were two of us on payroll. I was heading to an area with no cell service and nothing to do. I had seen the writing on the wall. Summers are tough for crowd-funded organizations. But I wasn't expecting this. What would we do?

I prayed a lot, made some phone calls, had our first-ever fundraising event, and by November we had close to fifty thousand dollars in the bank! Here's the takeaway. Every time our mettle is tested and we choose the path of courage, we grow stronger. When we tap out, we become weaker and more cowardly. Resistance only makes you weaker when you tap out or refuse to fight against it. But it makes you stronger when you press against it.

I recently climbed Oregon's' third highest mountain, the South Sister, with my son, Darby. With 4,900 feet of vertical gain in only six miles (one way) it is a total grind. I was one of the oldest people summiting the mountain that day and outweighed everyone by well over 30 pounds. Darby was worried. I was barely moving. I wanted to tap. All I had to do was point my hips home and downhill. I was cramping. It was brutal.

But I made it. I have the pictures to prove it!

Darby, who runs half marathons as working out said something very profound: "Dad I have never seen you struggle so much to do something. It was awesome. I'm proud of you."

I became strong in his eyes. It reminded me of what Abraham Lincoln (1809–1865) once said: "Impossibilities vanish when a man and his God confront the mountain."

Every act of courage is sign of strength to those who witness it, just as every act of apathy is seen as weakness.

RIVER CROSSINGS

A while back I was the keynote speaker for a men's weekend in the Blue Mountains east of Milton-Freewater, Oregon. As excited as I was to speak about biblical masculinity, I was almost as excited for the mountain biking trip on the final day. A handful of us would ride along the Blue Mountains, drop into South Fork Canyon, cross the Walla Walla River, and ride into Walla Walla, Washington. The trip would be an epic 35 miles long with an 8-mile descent into South Fork Canyon to the Walla Walla River.

It was a ride I'll never forget. With the Eastern Oregon springs come lush foliage, snow runoff, and crisp mountain air. The downhill was one of the most epic ones of my life, but the highlight for me was the unexpected river crossing that nobody warned me about.

The Walla Walla during the spring runoff is a cold, fast-moving river, nearly four feet deep in places, and 30 yards across. We skidded to a stop at the riverbank, and my first thought was, "How will we ever get across that raging river?" Remember, we were wearing mountain biking shoes, which have extremely stiff plastic soles and very little traction. They are awkward to walk in under normal circumstances, let alone when crossing an angry river.

Before I could ask the question, the local guys started taking off their shoes for the crossing. That answered my question. This would be a barefoot crossing. I was too frightened to hesitate and too prideful to ask questions. It was go-time. The only other option was 8 miles back up the mountain. *No gracias*. We were all in. Courage was the only choice. I hoped I'd survive it.

Besides one incident where I slipped, submerged my bike, and drifted downstream for a bit, we made it across no worse for the wear, but much wetter.

We've come to the river crossing of this book.

We're at the end of the book and are staring at a raging river to the other side and wondering, "How do I get across? What do I do next?"

The good news is that you aren't alone. I've crossed this river before and know the way across. I'm taking my shoes off as we speak. I'd be honored to guide you. I'm not talking about a literal river anymore. I'm talking about you becoming the best version of a man during your busy life and the many demands placed upon you. You are already a good man, which is what motivated you to pick up this book in the first place. Let us help you become a great one and a hero to the family that God has asked you to lead. I'm not perfect but I have been across the river and can show you the way.

At Men in the Arena we have four simple steppingstones to get you across the river to your best self. Here they are.

Steppingstone #1. Follow us.

Do this by going to our website and getting our free download. It will be easily located on our home page www.meninthearena.org. When you do, we will add you to our weekly equipping blast for men. The equipping blast is the best free resource out there to help you become your best version. This book is another resource, and you already have it. See, you've already jumped onto one stone and only have three more to go.

We regularly offer books from our many guest authors on the Men in the Arena Podcast. When you do visit us online you should join the Men in the Arena Army with access to our Facebook forum, podcast, and tons of free resources to help you cross the river. By "join" I mean subscribe to one or all of our free resources: weekly Equipping Blast, Men in the arena Podcast, and Facebook Forum for men only. You can also follow me at @jimwramos. I post about manhood daily. It's an easy way to stay connected.

Take the free online Best Version Assessment on our website and see how you measure up. It is a shortened version that will give you an actual number and percentage ranking based on the manhood essentials discussed in depth in my book, *Strong Men Dangerous Times*, combined with the 20 Qualifications for Spiritual Leaders found in the Pastoral Epistles of the Bible: 1 Timothy. 2 Timothy, and Titus. The assessment is designed to help applaud your strengths and reveal your blind spots. This assessment will be the most detailed resource for measuring your growth as you strive to become your best version.

If you want a more detailed analysis, make sure to pick up a copy of the *Full Capacity Man* to be released in June of 2022. In it are 200 assessing statements that will give you a detailed look at your strengths and weaknesses

Steppingstone #2. Invest in our resources.

If you haven't visited our website, go back to Steppingstone #1. Do that first. This will give you full access to the Men in the Arena world. If this book has resonated with your masculine DNA, then pick up another one of our resources and continue on the journey to the best you. We believe we have some of the best small group resources for men on the market and would love to help you start a group of your own. Let us know how we can help you.

If you move fast, you can book me as a keynote speaker for your church, men's event or leadership seminar and I will fly the books to you. You can find out more about my fees, calendar, and topics on our website.

Steppingstone #3. Join (or start) a team.

We passionately believe that the **greatest** steppingstone of all is when men lock shields with other men in a safe environment where you can ask questions, be encouraged, confess sin, and receive prayer. True life change happens there. Our virtual teams are led by our amazing volunteer National Team Captains. We have witnessed man after man becoming his best version through our small groups. You can easily sign up on our website.

Our resources are simple and easy to use for the guy who lives a full life. Being in a small group in the greatest decision you will ever make. Don't cross the river alone!

Steppingstone #4. Tell us your story.

This our favorite part. We are all on a journey, but you will cross to the other side sooner than you think. When you experience a life changing moment, we want to celebrate it with you. Every week we post at least one "Hero Story" on our Equipping Blast. We have no other way to capture the victories except through you sharing your story. When a man gets it—everyone wins!

It's that simple. Go to our website and pick up the free download, then buy one of our resources, start (join) a team, and tell us your story. Thank you for taking the time to enjoy one of our resources.

We are humbled and blessed.

"One man with courage makes a majority."
—Andrew Jackson (1767–1845)

About the Author

Thank you for taking your precious time to read this book.

I am honored and hope you were inspired and encouraged on the journey towards your best version. Lets lock arms on our journey. You can follow my journey on Facebook, Twitter, or Instagram @jimwramos.

As you've probably realized from many pages in this book, I have been married to my beautiful bride Shanna since 1992. She's the most important person in my life. We love drinking coffee, traveling to tropical places, and eating out with friends.

I'm first and foremost a follower of Jesus. I am a husband, father, grandfather. I am an avid book reader, fitness lover, and outdoorsman. My passion is hunting with my sons and a select few hunting partners.

I love hanging out with men over a Café Americano and learning their story. You can learn more about my story at the meninthearena.org

When a man gets it—everyone wins.

Made in the USA
Monee, IL
03 March 2022

92239258R00127